Einstein said that if you raise the quality of your thinking, you also raise the quality of your life and most problems will just fade away or disappear. As I became determined to go to any lengths to beat my addictions, I discovered the sure way to decrease their power was to stop entertaining thoughts for the poisons, which took up so much space in my mind. I came to believe that thought always comes before action and I finally recognized the truth: because of my thinking, I was the problem. I had to change my attitude, change my habits, change my friends and above all, change my thoughts.

Each day, I practiced for an hour to ignore and dispose of the control of these poisonous thoughts. My lies that I could not stop drinking, smoking or using drugs, originated from the thoughts of my old diet. My new diet fed me the truth and gave me the wisdom and strength to overpower and dispose of the lies and the addictions.

No one else can do it for you. You might start the whole process by asking for God's help. It's not necessary to understand God at this time, I couldn't. At first I could not pray, be honest or sincere when I started talking to him but he taught me how to speak the language of the heart and to try to be the best I could be. I found a degree of truth, honesty, love, and freedom with his help and on that shaky foundation I built a new life. After twenty-seven years free of alcohol, drugs, tobacco and other addictions, I am convinced I made a great investment.

As a counsellor and therapist I have been fortunate to have the opportunity to use and try different programs and methods during my Twelve Step work for a good recovery not only for myself, but also for others. I now hope you or any other addict would like to try my Do It Yourself Project. I have had thousands of letters, cards, and messages telling me it works. If it worked for us, it will work for you. The results speak louder than words and the only cost will be an open mind and a little bit of your time each day. What have you got to lose?

Last week I invited my wife out for dinner and a movie; the movie was *A Beautiful Mind*. It is the true story of John Nash, a professor at Princeton University. He was a victim of schizophrenia, a terrible disease that gave him visions of people in his mind, giving him problems and pain until he learned to ignore and replace these visions so that they could not harm him anymore. The students and faculty had a lot of laughs at his expense, but he faced and overcame this disease that had destroyed so many thousands of victims. In 1994, John Nash was awarded the Nobel Prize in Economics, becoming an inspiration to others to use their minds in seeking a cure or a miracle.

I am not ashamed to admit that I cried at times through the movie and I could relate with what Nash went through to get well. See the movie *A Beautiful Mind* and you will also be inspired. John Nash has confirmed and strengthened my faith in the power of God and the power of the mind. You have the power, don't waste it.

Your Friend,
Mike Maloney

THE
ROAD
TO
HELL

AND BACK

MICHAEL MALONEY

ELTON-WOLF PUBLISHING

THE ROAD TO HELL

AND BACK

Cover design by David Marty
Text design by Monica Nieman

Published by Elton-Wolf Publishing
Seattle, Washington

ISBN: 1-58619-037-7
Library of Congress Catalog Number:
2002102295

First Edition printed in May 2002
Printed in Canada

ELTON-WOLF PUBLISHING
2505 Second Avenue Suite 515   Seattle, Washington 98121
Tel 206.748.0345 Fax 206.748.0343
www.elton-wolf.com info@elton-wolf.com
Seattle • Los Angeles

DEDICATION

I dedicate this book

to the millions of alcohol and drug addicts

who have been deceiving themselves

into believing that they can't stop

drinking or using drugs,

and who have never understood

the power of the mind.

ACKNOWLEDGMENTS

I would like to thank all those wonderful people who helped me face my responsibilities and become accountable for my problems and my many defects of character.

I would especially like to thank the Twelve Steps of Alcoholics Anonymous that I had to force-feed to myself. My efforts seemed hopeless at first but I made a list of my assets and liabilities and prayed for the courage to keep going. I soon found people who were put in my path and who made my repair job so much easier.

Dr. Don M. in Montreal, Roy S. and Bill N. also from Montreal. The late Basil Smith of Ottawa's St. Patrick's Church, Scottie H. of Vancouver, The Maple Leaf Farm in Vermont, and the Maple Ridge Treatment Centre in British Columbia where I completed my first Five Steps.

The late Lillian Avery who bought me my first dictionary and kept insisting that I write a book, and my wonderful wife, Margaret, without whom I could never have finished it. Also the greatest person who ever lived, my dear Mother who contributed the example of courage and patience in my troubled life. I dedicate this book to her memory and pray we will meet again and continue to share our love.

I wish I could thank everyone that has helped me personally but I am sure they will be rewarded by finding their dreams. God Bless.

Mike Maloney

ACKNOWLEDGMENT TO THE ALCOHOLICS ANONYMOUS TWELVE STEP PROGRAM

A big reason for writing this book was a statement that Bill Wilson, founder of Alcoholics Anonymous, wrote on page 147 of his book *As Bill Sees It*.

We can be grateful for every agency or method that tries to solve the problem of Alcoholism, whether of medicine, religion, education or research. We can be open-minded towards all such efforts, and we can be sympathetic when the ill-advised ones fail. We can remember that Alcoholics Anonymous itself ran for years on trial and error. As individuals we can and should work with those that promise success— even a little success.

My experiences in Alcoholics Anonymous and the practice of the Twelve Steps, introduced me to a new way of life that allowed me to release and dispose of the garbage in my mind. The chance to refill my head with quality thoughts and actions will keep me forever grateful and indebted to this wonderful program.

You may come across some lines or phrases that are repeated, but I can assure you, they need repeating.

CONTENTS

INTRODUCTION TO MY FAMILY

I learned from the Twelve Steps of Alcoholics Anonymous that I had to play with the cards that were dealt to me even if they were stacked against me. I was descended from a line of alcoholics: grandfather, father. When I added alcohol, drugs, and toxic friends to this type of homebrew, it produced a madman who was irresponsible and unpredictable.

I was poorly prepared to be a husband and father with the responsibility of providing for and bringing up seven children. My own father had fifteen children, five died before their fifteenth birthday and there was many a time I wished I was one of them.

In my struggle for survival and a good life, I began to think that a good woman like my wonderful Mom, whom I considered a saint, could be very helpful in my recovery. I met and married Doris but I always treated her the same way as my father treated my Mother, like a slave. I feel sick when I realize how I acted and all I put that wonderful girl through. She produced seven healthy beautiful children who never had a chance to remain healthy because of the tyrant who claimed to be their father. I was the worst thing that could have happened to them. I always hated myself for the way I was. I seriously tried to end my life by committing crimes hoping to attract a police bullet.

Our first child was born in 1948, he was a healthy and happy baby. Doris was seventeen and I was twenty-one. We placed him on a farm with a nice couple and we agreed to pay them each month as we traveled around selling magazines. It was a good arrangement for us at that time. In the next fifteen years three daughters and three sons were born. All this time I was at my worst. I was being arrested often and thrown in jail, and could not stay away from the booze. I had also begun to have blackouts. After a few drinks I would not know what I was doing. The next day when I was told what I had done the night before, I could not believe it. There were many times when I must have been completely out of my mind. I can't imagine what I put my wife and children through during this period of their lives.

My father had introduced all his kids to terror and a living hell, and now it was my turn. I began to hate myself and blame my wife and kids for all my problems. For me, living was worse than dying. It is very hard to write about this period of my life because there is no way that I can escape the memories or heartaches I caused my family.

In 1992, after seventeen years completely free of alcohol and drugs, with a certificate as a counsellor and therapist and a practice in Ottawa, I received a shock that nearly sent me back. My second son, whom I truly loved, and who had gone to bat for me a few times, died of an overdose of heroin. I was heartbroken. I had taken him to several A.A. and N.A. meetings hoping he would go back to the meetings on his own and continue with the program. He was thirty-eight years old, and left behind a beautiful wife and a great little son. The year before when I became ill and could have lost my employment agency in Ottawa, I called him in Montreal and told him I was in the hospital. Two days later he was at my bedside with the money I needed to see me through. In 1996, just four years later, my second daughter, age forty-four with three children, also died from an overdose. She had planned to visit me that summer in Ottawa. We talked on the phone often and we were so excited about seeing each other, but I guess it wasn't meant to be.

I have a good relationship with three of my remaining children who live close by, and I have found a wonderful wife whom I married two years ago. Although we are in our mid-seventies, we make the most of each day. When I escaped from my hell, I never dreamed that I could find a little bit of heaven for my remaining years, but I have, and you can too.

When I started this book my plan was to try to understand the reasons and find the answers for my own failures and problems so that my children might learn something from my experiences and mistakes and I could be a good example for my children. But before I could finish this book and try to make amends, the ones who needed it most were gone. I put the book aside for several years never expecting to finish it, but there are many people who need help with their addictions, and by telling my story, they might want to try my "do-it-yourself project."

March 30, 2002 will be my twenty-seventh anniversary without a drink or a drug. I am sure that if I can do it, anybody can—with the help of

God, a belief in yourself, and the Twelve Steps. My greatest wish is that this book helps you to find your correct path through life before it's too late.

CHAPTER ONE

WHAT IT WAS LIKE

The year was 1934, the city was Montreal. I was seven years old. I awoke to the sound of footsteps over my head, shivering because I should have found more newspapers to wrap around me. There was about two feet of space between the ground and the veranda under which I was sleeping. When I had enough papers round me I was usually quite warm. The newspapers served a double purpose. There were a lot of mice and rats in my neighbourhood and although many a night I fell asleep watching them, they never bothered me. I think the rattling of the paper must have kept them away. I realize this now, but at the time I liked to believe that they accepted me as just another dumb animal, and since I was no threat to them, they left me alone.

Before this, I had been sleeping in the stairways or the hallways of apartment buildings but the police spotted me a couple of times and took me home where my old man beat the hell out of me, leaving me bruised and hurting for days. I would run away again the first chance I got because I knew my father hated me. I never did find out why. I was always so terrified of him and so full of fear that I could not stay around him for any length of time. I was the fourteenth of fifteen children. Two had passed away at a young age leaving five brothers and eight sisters. Three of these were to pass away in the next few years and by the time I was fifteen, there were ten of us left. I know now that my father should never have had any children as he was an alcoholic. My dear Mother just didn't have time for us all. She worked as a scrub woman for a dollar a day during the Depression, just to feed us.

When I left my sleeping quarters under the veranda, it was to begin my daily forage for food. I was born in 1927 just in time for the Great Depression. In the 1930s milk and bread were delivered to nearly every doorstep. Knowing my district well, I knew exactly when the milkman delivered his milk and when the bread man delivered his bread, so it was easy to grab some food to start off the day. Occasionally there was also a pound of butter or a bottle of chocolate milk that I really appreciated. I would often watch the milkman take a note from the bottle and read it, then leave a little something extra—eggs, butter, cream. I would follow him and steal whatever he left.

After I had eaten, I headed for the train tracks where I knew my chances for lunch were good because I had some resourceful friends at the "Old Mill," which was just a burnt-out building. It had no roof and half the walls were gone, but I treasure the memories of the food I shared with the hobos who sheltered there, and the wonderful stories they told me about faraway places and other hobo jungles they had visited across the United States and Canada. I'll always be grateful for having met those wonderful people.

I think this was the first time that an adult sat and talked to me as an equal. Most adults, at least the ones I had known, seemed to believe children should be seen and not heard, and yet these people seemed to be genuinely concerned about my problems. More importantly, they seemed to understand me.

Many times later in my life, my experiences

with social workers, doctors, counselors, etc. left me feeling discouraged because I could not seem to get through to them. I am convinced today that my hobo friends knew how I felt and could relate to me because, like them, I was an outcast trying to survive.

I remember the way they made out their shopping list for the things they would need for the day. Each hobo received his assignment; one would get the potatoes, one the carrots, another the meat, onions, etc. and one would be responsible for cooking it all. The meal usually ended up as a potpourri of anything that was edible, and I remember the excitement rising as the feast began. I'll never forget having to find an old jar or tin can in which to receive my portion. I never heard any complaints about the food. I guess the hungrier you are the better the food tastes. I can't remember how long I enjoyed the hobos' hospitality before I decided to accept some responsibility and do my share by bringing bread, milk, butter, or whatever I could lay my hands on. For the first time in my life, I was being complimented and accepted. They really seemed to care how I felt.

I spent many happy hours listening to hobo tales of good times and travels. Most were optimists, and left me with the impression that tomorrow belonged to them, if only they could hang in there today. There were sad times as well. I would get really close to one of them and all of a sudden he would leave. I was always a sensitive kid, and terribly shy. I took a while to make friends and it seemed that no sooner did I have a good friend than I lost him. This played havoc with my emotions. Some friends would go east, some would go west, and even though as they left, I knew that I would never see them again, there were always new hobos and new stories.

Some would arrive all bruised and battered from the beatings they had taken from some railroad cop. It was not hard to believe the stories of brutality and pain a lot of these people endured, even though their only crime was stealing a ride on a freight train to another city, hoping to find some work. One cop, the most sadistic bastard of them all, was called Capreol Red. Capreol was a railroad town in northern Ontario, not far from Sudbury, Ontario. Capreol Red beat some of the hobos so severely they died. Others wore the scars of his fists and boots for the rest of their lives. I saw the results of his beatings—you would think the victims had been mauled by a bear. Hobos so feared this maniac they would get off the freight train before it got to Capreol and skirt the town on foot. When they thought they were at a safe distance, they would catch another freight.

I have fond memories of those wonderful people I met, and I consider my life so much richer for having met them. Some call them the dregs of society. Well, I have met many supposed pillars of society and men of the cloth and, believe me, there is more understanding, trust, consideration, kindness and love among those hobos. As time goes by I value the experiences I shared with those unfortunate people more and more.

I am sure the reason I liked my new friends so much was that living at home was like living in a lion's den or hornet's nest. I remember fighting for my share of food and not always getting it. I can remember the day my Mom, when she went out working, left a large can of beans for our lunch. We ran the six blocks from school so that we could get our share, only to run into the kitchen to find an empty can because my older brother Bob had opened it and eaten all the beans cold. Bob was big for his age and always hungry; we all hated him that day. I did not return to school that day because my choices were going back to school hungry or finding something to eat. My instinct for self-preservation won out as usual and I quickly learned to survive on my own.

One of the earliest money-making scams my kid sister and I started around that time was selling tickets on a big beautiful doll. It started when a girl and a boy about ten or eleven years old came to our door with raffle tickets and a lovely doll in a box. The tickets were priced from one cent to ten cents. You would pick a folded ticket, unfold it and pay whatever amount was on the ticket in order to get a chance to win the doll. Although we had no money to buy a ticket for ourselves, we thought it was a great idea, so we tried to improve on it. We made up one hundred tickets from one cent to ten cents, in bunches of ten which amounted to five dollars and fifty cents. We could not buy a doll so we got a catalogue and cut out two pictures of beautiful dolls. I'll never forget our first sale. A woman picked a ticket marked three cents. She gave us three pennies, and we became so excited, we took off before she had time to close the door.

We raced to the candy store and I can still remember what we bought—two honeymoons, two coconut balls, and a peppermint stick. We went back to work and decided to knock on doors until we collected a quarter in change. We really thought we could buy a doll but we never could save the five dollars that it cost. We told people that the money was for the poor, and since you could not find anyone much poorer than us, it actually was the truth!

I hated school. It seems the truant officer was always looking for me. He found me a few times but I usually outran him. I can remember being humiliated when my father took me back to school on a leash. He had a long belt that he tied around my wrist and literally dragged me. I guess I should be grateful it wasn't around my neck. The kids all laughed and thought it very funny. I thought it unfair that when the old man caught me doing something wrong, he took me home and beat the hell out of me, then dragged me to school where I got the strap again.

Oh, how happy I was when he took off for Detroit or some other city looking for work. Then I could sleep at home and not worry about him coming home drunk. There was always a lot of celebrating as soon as he left town and the atmosphere around the house improved.

My parents were both brought up on farms in Quebec. They met one day, got married and found a farm of their own. They never seemed to have enough food for a growing family, so they moved to Montreal; but there it was even worse. My old man couldn't find work, and he became more frustrated and meaner as the years went by. There were many times I wished I had not been born. My parents were Catholics, thought their children were sent by God, so did not believe in birth control. The teachings of their church played a cruel joke on them.

My parents were as different as night and day. They both believed in God but their conceptions of God were entirely different although, at the time it was hard for me to distinguish the difference between their gods. My old man was very religious. He was on his knees morning and night. He went to church every Saturday and Sunday and raised hell the rest of the week. He believed that he was free to do whatever he wanted during the week, as long as he confessed his sins on the weekend.

On Saturday he would come home from confession, throw my Mother down two flights of stairs, then the following morning he'd walk piously down the centre aisle of the church with his hands folded, ready to kneel and take communion. Worse yet, he made us take communion as well. I had a hard time to keep from puking. Oh, how I hated that old hypocrite! I could never stand being in the same room or house with him. If something went wrong when I was around, he always found some way to blame it on me and give me a beating, which is why I took off every chance I got.

My Mom was also a religious person, but with a beautiful conception of God. Her belief was simple—she believed that if you did what was right, God would be with you and you would prosper; if you did what was wrong, he would stay away and you would suffer. Her God was kind, considerate, forgiving, understanding, and, most of all, loving.

My darling Mom had more faith than anyone I have ever met. She would leave home in the morning and go out to work for a dollar a day scrubbing walls, ceilings, and floors. There were very few eight-hour days. She started at seven or eight in the morning and finished when her employers let her go, but her day's work never seemed to end. As soon as she got home she had all the housework to do. My sisters never helped much. Their attitude was, Mom can do it! I know I also took advantage of Mom's goodness. We all did. Rather than argue, poor darling Mom just went ahead and did it.

There were some things I could never understand about my Mom such as the times in the middle of the night when I went to use the bathroom, and found her bent over a bathtub full of dirty clothes, scrubbing them on a scrub board. Despite this she was always humming and seemed to be happy. She had this great faith in God and her favourite saint was the Mother of Perpetual Help and her favourite expression was: "There is more wrought by prayer than this world dreams of."

The happiest days I ever had as a child were when Mom did not have to go to work and we spent the day together. Up until age six or seven, there were no toys that I can remember, but she could make simple little things seem important and keep me busy for much of the time. She'd give me an old newspaper and a pair of scissors, and ask me to make small pieces of paper, pretending that she needed them. She would show me how to cut a long strip of the paper and then cut it into small pieces. Every time I filled up a small box, she made a big deal of it and gave me a hug and a kiss and some small reward such as a piece of bread and peanut butter. But the most important thing was that she made me feel needed, wanted, and loved.

My father always told me that I was no good, never had been any good, and never would be any good. Mom kept telling me that things would get better, and I believed her because I loved her and knew she wouldn't lie to me. He was the devil on earth, she surely was a saint. Before I started to run away from home I spent more nights under the bed and hiding in the closets than I did in bed. Fear was not something that happened to me once in a while—it was a permanent state of mind.

My eldest brother, Cyril, whom we called Cy, was twenty-one years older than me. He had a drinking problem that turned into a serious drug problem. He played junior hockey as a teenager until he got kicked in the leg but he didn't see a doctor or go to the hospital because he didn't think it was serious. Gangrene set in and he had to have his lower leg removed. After the operation the surgeons discovered that they hadn't stopped the infection, so they removed the rest of his leg up to the hip.

Cy was a good hustler. He could raise a buck when no one else could, but he was always on booze or drugs. Coming home from a beer parlour late one night he was struck by a trolley car and nearly killed. He was in the hospital for a couple of months and when he came out he was hooked on morphine. At first he conned the doctors into prescribing it, but as his addiction increased, he had to depend on drug pushers.

He used to phone a small pharmacy about six blocks from home and send me with a note to pick up small packets of white powder. Only later did I learn that it was morphine. I was a drug-runner at eight years of age. I watched as he prepared the fix by placing the powder on a spoon and adding a little water, bringing this to a boil, sucking it up in a syringe, tapping the syringe with his finger to get rid of any air bubbles, wrapping a tie or piece of tubing around his arm to make the veins pop out, and then ending the ritual by sticking the needle in a vein, depressing the plunger, and waiting a few seconds for blastoff.

Around this time the old man was often leaving town to look for work. He would take off whenever he heard there might be work available in Toronto, Detroit, or Chicago. It was also around this time that I first got arrested for stealing empty bottles. I could climb like a monkey from veranda to veranda, from roof to roof, and I knew the alleys like the back of my hand. I usually outran the cops unless they came upon me by surprise. This time they waited until I went into the store to sell the bottles. They came in behind me, grabbed me and took me off to juvenile court. I stayed there about a week, received a suspended sentence, and was told not to steal anymore.

Shortly after this, my old man returned and I hit the road again. I was sure in my mind that he would go into one of his rages and kill us all and I didn't want to be around when that happened. I went back to my outdoor life and began picking up bread and milk for breakfast and occasionally a pound of butter if I got lucky.

One day at Mary's Restaurant, a real greasy spoon on the main street where I hung around, I asked Mary if she would buy some butter from me for half–price. At the time it was twenty cents a pound and I offered to get it for ten cents. She promised to take all I could get. You must bear in mind that during the Great Depression you could get a good grocery order for one dollar. Hamburger was three pounds for a quarter, sausages were the same price, potatoes were ten pounds for a nickel, a loaf of bread was about seven cents, an ice cream cone was two cents, and a bottle of cola pop was three cents, so a dime could go a long way.

This was the first time that I went out to hustle a buck on my own. I soon found that walking up and down streets searching for butter was doing it the hard way and concluded that if people could put a note in their milk bottles and get a pound of butter, then so could I. So I started to write notes the night before, asking the milkman to leave butter, or whatever I could get. I spread my notes a respectable distance apart so as not to arouse suspicion, and changed areas often to avoid hitting the same milkman more than once.

But even the best-laid plans can go awry. I had been working a high-class district where I thought they would not notice a pound of butter on their weekly milk bill. But one morning after about six months I walked up to a beautiful house and, as I bent to pick up the butter, the door burst open and a cop grabbed me! I was really shocked, and the experience scared me so much that I could never steal from a doorstep again.

I was taken by the police to juvenile court and the following day passed in front of Judge Robinette. My poor wonderful Mom was there. It broke my heart to see the anguish on her face and the tears that flowed as she pleaded with the judge to give me just one more chance. She told him that I was a good boy, that I didn't mean to do anything wrong, and that if he gave me just one more chance I would never do it again. She really believed what she was saying. I know she convinced me!

Before I went in front of the judge, I told her to please tell him that I was a Protestant, so that I could go to Shawbridge Boys' Farm up in the mountains where the kids were treated well and there were lots of sports and recreation, but Mom could not deny her religion so she told the court that I was a Catholic. I was sentenced to the École de Réforme Mont St-Antoine (reform school) for a period of five years. The curriculum consisted of courses in violence, hate, anger, frustration, lies, fear, confusion, to name a few. I went in an amateur and came out a professional, ready to ply my new trade.

CHAPTER TWO

REFORM SCHOOL

The École de Réforme Mont St-Antoine was the greatest preparatory school for criminals ever created. I was told stories about this place and had been warned about the special treatment you received if you were English-speaking. I was sent along with three French-speaking kids to the reform school that same afternoon, and I can truthfully say that until then that was the worst day of my life. First of all, I was ten years old; when you're ten, and you know that five years is half your lifetime, a five-year sentence seems like an eternity. There is no way I can describe the horrible feelings I had that day.

When we arrived they took us to a room and read us the Riot Act, the Do's and Don'ts, the

23

Rules, and the rest. I could not understand what was being said, so I made my first big mistake—I asked a question in English. The brother took a fit and started screaming at me. The only words I could pick out were *maudit bloke*, because I had heard this on the streets quite often. That was an important lesson—*maudit bloke* meant damned Englishman. The French always used this phrase when arguing with the English. Any kid brought up in Montreal in those days knew what *maudit bloke* meant. The French kids asked questions and got civil answers, but as soon as I opened my mouth, and spoke the dreaded English, all hell broke loose. I was very careful from then on, and I spoke as little as possible whenever the Great Men were around.

My name was Earl at that time, and Earl is about the hardest name to pronounce in French. They usually just called me *le bloke* or *maudit bloke*. Later, because of the way I crashed out of there they gave me the nickname, "The Crasher." I was glad when the kids gave me this nickname because my real name was Valentine Aloyiousius Earl Maloney. I was born on Valentine's Day; that is where I got Valentine. My godfather was an Irish priest by the name of Aloyiousius, and the governor-general of Canada at that time was the

Earl of Athlone; so that is how I got stuck with those names.

At home I was called Earl, but as I said earlier, that is about the most difficult name to pronounce in French. Some called me Ull, others Oui and Oil. Anyway, I had never liked my names. It was bad enough being born the fourteenth of fifteen children, without having to be given such lousy names, which is why I traded them all for Mike.

There were over five hundred kids in this place. There were four big rooms called "halls." There was one for the kids ten years of age and under; Medium B was for kids ten to twelve; Medium C was for kids twelve to fourteen; and the big hall was for kids fourteen and over. There were approximately one hundred and twenty-five kids per room, five or six of whom were English-speaking kids from Irish, Polish, Italian, and Native Indian families. We were all considered "blokes."

That first day was hell on earth. My Mother's face, with tears running down her cheeks, kept appearing in my thoughts and I hated myself so much for the heartache I had caused her. I will never forget that beautiful, kind, tender, loving face as long as I live. I thank God for giving me the greatest Mother any kid ever had.

The whole first month was bad. I couldn't adjust, and I soon realized that there was no hope of my ever adjusting as long as I continued to speak English. I'd once heard a song that I could really relate to; the lines went something like: "You just got to know the language." In my case this was true. It soon became obvious that the less I said, the better my chances were of staying out of trouble, but I was in a no-win situation. I was damned if I did and damned if I didn't. I started believing that I was "no good," just as my father had said.

I was confused for I don't know how long. The harder I tried to adjust, the more confused I became. I was always a very emotional kid and could not stop crying. I hated anyone seeing me crying, but the only privacy I could get in the day-time was the bathroom—and even there I could not be alone, since there were always other kids around. It was a great relief to get into bed at night, cover up my head, and be alone with my thoughts, imagining that I was home with Mom. As I was falling asleep I would hear her saying: "It's all right, son, everything is going to be all right. Things will get better." But in reality things got a lot worse.

I started school right away, and was put in a

classroom with about thirty other kids. I was also given a pencil, school books and copy books, but they didn't do me much good because they were all in French. The idiot who was supposed to be a teacher taught me lessons I will never forget: frustration, depression, humiliation, and hate. Especially hate. I hadn't expected to find anyone that I could hate more than my father, but this teacher taught me how. I remember being punished, and not knowing what I had done wrong. I was also taught how to scheme and lie. I became an accomplished liar.

The teacher would give the class some lessons in French, and he expected me to understand and keep up with the rest. If I couldn't he gave me the strap; he used that strap so often on me that it hurt less and less as time went by. He also liked humiliating me in front of the other kids. They all looked at me and laughed as though I were some kind of freak. I became very self-conscious, much more of a loner, and I think my hate increased as I tried to use it to shield myself from a lot of physical and mental pain. I am, and always will be, convinced that those teachers got their kicks from being cruel. Many of them were nothing less than sadistic bastards enjoying their power over us.

The staff of the reform school were all broth-

ers belonging to some religious order, and they
went to church morning, noon, and night, dragging
us kids along with them. Each brother wore a large
rosary and cross around his waist, and another
cross hung around his neck. And they all wore that
holier-than-thou look, the look I had first seen on
my old man's face. I often thought, "Who the hell
do they think they are kidding?"

They had types and degrees of punishment
that would have made the Marquis de Sade envious. If a kid ran away, or got caught trying, they
had a number of special punishments—the
banan, the *cachot*, and the *carabole*. The *banan*
was a piece of leather about three feet long and
twice as thick as a garden hose. It was filled with
sand, and was most effective in discouraging kids
from sitting down. It left your ass in a terrible
mess. Kids who got the *banan* had red and blue
welts for weeks after, and quickly learned to
sleep on their stomachs. Some of the kids showed
me their asses after they got the *banan*, and the
sight made me sick, not to mention the added fear
it created in me.

We kids had to stand at attention in the big
room and listen to each stroke of the *banan*, the
terrifying screams of pain and the crying and
pleading for mercy. I am sure that every kid who

heard this was affected by it. I could never understand why people started an association to protect
animals—The Society for the Prevention of
Cruelty to Animals—and did not give the same
protection to children. At the time, in that
province, the Church was more powerful than the
government, so I guess the Church and its affiliat-
ed branches could do no wrong.

Cachot is French for dungeon. The reform
school's *cachot* was a small room with no furniture. Six inches off the floor was a wooden
platform for a bed, and in the corner was a pail for
a toilet. There was so much darkness and silence,
it might as well have been a real dungeon. The
standard sentence was eight days, and, strange as
it may sound, I never looked forward to getting
out. That's because I received twelve shots of the
banan before going in, and another twelve when I
got out. My ass would be raw for days, and just
knowing that they were going to give me another
beating before I'd recovered from the last one was
like living a nightmare.

In the *cachot* I slept in fits and starts, and
when they came around with bread and water I
was too scared to eat. I didn't know if it was night
or day because my cell was dark all the time. I
only knew it was another day when they brought

my bread and water. On the dreaded day of my release they gave me the *banan* again, followed by the *carabole*—they shaved all my hair off. I never understood why they added this extra punishment, unless it was to humiliate us. This was one time in my life that I remember feeling sorry for myself. People in the same circumstances who did not feel sorry for themselves had to be nuts.

An average day in the life of an inmate went like this: you rose at six-thirty, made your bed, washed, dressed and stood by your bed for inspection. The brothers checked your bed and your appearance, and if they found something wrong they made you stand by the washroom. After the other kids went to chapel, you got the strap. After chapel you went to the refectory, where you and the other kids sat ten to a table and shared the rations, which consisted of bread, a pot of grease, a bowl of mustard, and black tea. The grease was hard and grey in colour with black spots. The kid at the head of the table cut the grease into ten pieces, one for each kid. We spread the grease on the dry bread, put mustard over it, and made a sandwich. We learned that it went down easier with lots of salt. There is one thing to say for this breakfast: nobody complained about not getting enough, and the brothers never had to worry about kids asking for seconds.

This was our diet every morning of the year except for Christmas, New Year's, Easter, and St. Jean-Baptiste Day, when these great holy men, out of the kindness of their hearts, presented us with a bun with real raisins and a whole cup of cocoa. It would be difficult to describe the slop they gave us at the other meals. The only thing I am sure of is that the best meal of the week was beans. We always looked forward to our feast of beans. They really did taste good, and we could see what we were eating.

The rest of our day was school, and after supper we went out into the yard to find something to do. Although there were gloves, balls, and bats, the brothers who handed them out always gave them to their darlings. Many of the brothers were homosexual, so when I came to know the system I did not even try to get the sports equipment. I stayed away from these creeps because if they did something for you—watch out. They would come around later to tell you that you owed them "a favour," and they would make sexual advances.

A lot of these holy men had their own special boys, usually the prettiest ones, and these couples were inseparable. Whenever you saw one you saw the other. I was also sexually abused by them. I would be awakened at two or three in the morning and told to come with them to their small room to talk. Before I knew it, their hands were all over me and I was paralyzed with fear at what they were doing to me. I can't believe, from the stories I have heard from other kids, that many inmates got through their sentences without being sexually assaulted.

The best part of our day was when we finally got to bed at night and could cover up our heads and relax in our own private worlds, with our own private thoughts. Mine were nearly always of home and my wonderful Mom. And then another day was gone, and I had only seventeen hundred and ninety-seven days left. I remember figuring out the number of days in five years, realizing that there were eighteen hundred and twenty-five, and each night thinking, "Well, one more day is gone." I was also beginning to think that home wasn't so bad after all. Compared to this, home was like staying at the Ritz Hotel.

Another thing that reform school taught me was that there is nothing so bad that it can't get worse. There were often times that I thought, "Well, I have really had it, it can't get any worse," but the next day I found out that it could, and usually did.

We were allowed one visitor a month. My section was called the "Small Hall," and the first Sunday of every month was our day. Oh, how we all looked forward to this special day! I had written to my Mom and told her that she could visit me, and she had written to say that she would be sure to be there, and that she would bring my sister Theresa, who was the youngest in the family. When the great day arrived I was very excited.

On visiting days, a boy came from the front office with a note for the brother-in-charge in our hall. The brother would ring a bell and call out a name. You could hear a pin drop, it was so quiet. Then some happy kid would run off to the visiting room. There was never a time in my life that I appreciated my Mom as much. I guess I had always taken her for granted, and had never realized how much I really loved her until I was locked up in there.

Well, my name was finally called, and although it was only a month since I had last seen her, it seemed like a year. She kept asking me what the place was like and I had to tell her a bunch of lies because I wanted to spare her feelings. There was no way that I could explain the holy men and their methods of teaching or their sadistic and homosexual practices. We were given one hour for our visit and there was no way I was going to ruin my happy hour by talking about their cruel and inhumane treatment.

Also, my Mom had great respect for men of the cloth, and it would have confused her all the more if I had tried to explain what was happening. I could not understand it, so I thought, "How could she?" She came alone to visit, and I was glad because I had her to myself for that hour. She once brought a rosary that she said was blessed, and a chocolate box with a pound of fudge in it. This was the first candy or sweets I'd had since before my arrest, and it didn't last long.

It's very hard for me to explain the reasoning behind some of the regulations and punishments they meted out. They seemed to defeat their own purpose with their straps and the *banan*. Although we all had an intense fear of this type of punishment at the beginning, the more they applied it to me the less I feared it. Eventually, my thinking changed and I was no longer afraid to run away because of the *banan*. What the hell; I was going to get it anyway, so what difference did it make? One good thing about getting it for running away was that you knew why you were getting it.

There were other punishments that filled me with hate. During the third month, for example, our visiting day rolled around again. I was excited and had been looking forward to it since my Mom last visited. It was the only day of the month that mattered, the only day that I could find a little bit of happiness. Visiting hours started at one o'clock and finished at four. Mom had told me in a letter that she would be early, and when two o'clock came without a call for me I started to worry. Then it was two-thirty, three, three-thirty and finally, four. My excitement had been gradually replaced by worry, fear, and sadness. My Mom had never before made a promise that she did not keep.

At about four-thirty they called my name and gave me a little package that my Mother had left for me. It was a small box of fudge with a note telling me how sorry she was that she could not see me, and explaining that they had told her I had lost my visiting privileges because I was bad. They had not said a word to me, and so I had not told her to not to bother coming. They seemed to enjoy handing out these kinds of surprises.

Another privilege that they offered us was a chance to go home for one day, once a month, after you were an inmate for at least three months. I tried my hardest to earn this privilege, but each month, when I looked at the blackboard to see if my name was there, I was disappointed. It was much later when I finally got a day's leave.

My old man never gave me a present of any kind in his life, but he once gave my brother Bob and me a present we could share—a set of boxing gloves. At that time the heavyweight champion of the world was an Irishman, James J. Braddock, and people were always talking about John L. Sullivan, a former world heavyweight champion, and Jimmy Maloney, who was a heavyweight contender at the time. My old man got the bright idea that he was going to train my brother and me to become professional boxers. I thought it was a good idea but I didn't realize what I was getting myself into.

Although my brother Bob was only a couple of years older than me, he was at least fifty pounds heavier. And three inches taller. While I weighed no more than one hundred pounds, my old man was at least two hundred. I can remember how frustrated I got because I could never win. I was born with a bad temper and a stubborn streak but these traits only made me hang in there longer and take more severe beatings. But there were a few lessons to be learned from boxing. I guess you could call this stage of my life, "learning the hard way."

One day when Bob was laying a good beating

on me, gloating and teasing at the same time, I was in such a rage that, as he came towards me with his legs spread just right and with the silly grin on his face that he always had when he was enjoying himself, I suckered him with a kick in the balls that I'm sure he remembered to his dying day. I will never forget the stunned look on his face and his moaning and groaning as he fell in a heap on the ground. I had found the equalizer, and I enjoyed every minute of his suffering. I had won my first fight with the gloves, and the taste of victory was so sweet that the boxing matches we had after that were much more fun, and a lot more even, because he was more cautious and well aware of my secret weapon.

My boxing experience with my brother and the old man came in handy at the reform school, because this was the only sport that I ever participated in there. My first fight came as a complete surprise. I returned to our hall after supper and was told by one of the kids that my name was up on the board and that I was going to fight an Italian kid. My first reaction was joy because I had no fear of fighting someone my size. In fact I thought it would be easy after fighting my brother and the old man.

I was a little disappointed because no one had

asked me if I wanted to fight, these arrogant bastards just told you what to do, and if you didn't do it you were punished. You had no choice. That first fight was a lot tougher than I thought it would be. We fought three three-minute rounds with one-minute rest periods between rounds and I won, but I sure knew that I had just been in a fight.

There are some basic rules that you should follow before a fight. You should train for it and you should not eat just before the match. I got sick to my stomach in the second round and wished that I hadn't eaten supper. Winning the fight brought me a little self-esteem, and some of the kids told me it was a good fight. The brother who was in my corner patted me on the back and said I had fought well. That was the first bit of praise or encouragement that I had received since setting foot in the place, and I loved it.

My name kept appearing on the blackboard night after night, and I kept fighting. I fell asleep each night dreaming of being the world champion and making so much money that my Mom would never have to work again. My family would be proud of me. At that time, boxing was the only profession by which an uneducated Irish kid from the other side of the tracks could reach the top. I was so determined to make it that my every moment was filled with thoughts and plans of how to beat the next guy.

Different brothers had been acting as corner men for my first five or six fights. Then I got lucky. There was a really nice brother called Frère Faustin, who was in charge of the change room. All the kids liked him, and he was always pleasant and happy. One particular night he was in my corner and, although he was not a very talkative person, he made me feel as if he cared about me.

He was only about five feet four inches tall and weighed maybe one hundred thirty-five pounds, but he was a giant as far as compassion, consideration and understanding went. He wiped my face with cold water between rounds, massaged my neck and shoulders, whispered words of encouragement, and at the same time looked out for bumps and bruises. I don't know where he came from, but nobody was ever appreciated more. Best of all, he wasn't homosexual. He and I became very good friends, and he always tried to help me.

One day at lunch hour when I was playing in the yard, and to this day I don't know what I did wrong, this pig, Frère Laurin, told me to go inside and wait at the washroom door for him. This creep weighed about two hundred and fifty pounds and was really ugly. He was the most feared and hated brother in the whole place, and when he picked you out for punishment you could be sure you were getting the *banan* because he never gave the strap on the hands, at least not to my knowledge.

He was the one who punished the kids who ran away, and he loved his work. I had seen many a kid who had been beaten by him—Frère Laurin was an expert at it. He affected every kid in the place. One minute a hundred kids would be playing in the great hall and the noise would be deafening, then all of a sudden the noise would subside and you could hear a pin drop. Sure enough, when you looked around, Frère Laurin had just entered the room.

I heard the bell ring outside and saw all the kids come marching in. When they saw a boy standing by the washroom door, they knew what he was there for. They had ten minutes to put their things away and use the toilet before the second bell, when they would line up and march off to their classes. Then when they were all gone Laurin would keep another brother behind to witness the punishment. These were the rules. You had to have a witness. I had been in for about six months and I still had a great fear of the *banan*.

Finally I was going to get it. Before the other

kids left for their classes a lot of them would pass close to me and give a few words of encouragement. Some asked what I did to deserve this and I swear to this day I don't know. The other kids warned me not to struggle or try to avoid it because kids who did always ended up getting more, especially on the upper legs or back.

When I went in I did exactly as I was told. I knelt down on the tile floor with my head between my hands and before I knew it, it was over. The only good thing about this punishment was that after the first whack your ass went so numb that the other whacks didn't hurt as much. The first shot was like an anaesthetic; it was like freezing a tooth. I found that the fear of the punishment was a lot worse than the punishment itself.

I had been initiated. It seems funny now as I reflect on it, but getting the *banan* was like getting a promotion to the ranks of the tougher, harder kids. Now I sat at the head of my table in the dining room, cut up the grease, and served myself first. There were other small privileges that went with my new status, such as having the kids share their presents from home with me. I became more popular and was proud to show the scars on my ass.

But what I experienced that day left me with

scars that I would never be able to show anyone: bitterness, hatred, fear, frustration. I hated my father for beating my Mom, hated the judge for sentencing me to five years, but this new hate that I had for this cowardly bastard in his religious robe was to stay with me for many years.

I went to see Frère Faustin, who was my good friend by now, and told him what had happened. I showed him my ass and asked him if he could find out why I got the *banan*. I thought that if I could find out why I got it, I could be careful not to do the same thing again. Oh, how I wish I had never mentioned it to Frère Faustin at all, because he spoke to Frère Laurin and Laurin told him more or less to mind his own business, adding that when he punished a boy, that boy deserved it.

I soon realized the grave error I had made in asking for Frère Faustin's help. The following Saturday afternoon, a friend and I were throwing a softball back and forth in the yard when the Pig came up behind me. Pig—that was one of our nicknames for Frère Laurin, although he was called a lot worse than that. He told me to go inside and wait for him, I went inside, and this time I was really scared. My ass was still aching from the last time he had give me the *banan*—the swelling had not even gone yet. You may have heard of people being worried sick; well, this was my first experience and it was worse than the punishment. I believe that is why they made us wait at the washroom door—so that we could run in and throw up if we had to.

Frère Laurin came in. Another brother was with him, so I knew I was to get the *banan* again. Laurin yelled and screamed in French, but the only part that I understood was that I was a *maudit menteur,* "damned liar," and that he was going to show me what happens to a damned liar. Well, I took my beating, and he left more scars on my ass, but I believe he left me so scarred mentally, that I will never be able to fully recover. I later tried to analyze his motives and came to three possible conclusions: he was a sadist and got sexual pleasure out of beating a kid's ass; he was a racist and hated anyone who spoke English; or he was just plain insane.

In retrospect, I can see that I was no model child or what some would call a "normal kid," but I knew right from wrong and I did expect to be punished when I did wrong; however, I thought the punishment should fit the crime. When I first got to reform school and compared my sentence with some of the other kids who had sentences of one, two or three years, it was obvious that my punishment did not fit my crime. Although the judge had said that he was going to make an example of me, this was bullshit because I knew of another kid from my district who had confessed to ten charges of breaking and entering and a lot of the stolen goods were found in his home. He only got three years. Any respect I had for the law vanished and was replaced by contempt.

When I got the *banan* for the second time in one week, for no logical reason, it just increased my hatred of authority and society. This may sound like self-pity, or self-dramatization but this is not so. I am trying to describe both the physical and mental pain. My ass was still swollen and hurting from the first time. It was like a washboard with welts and grooves. There were scabs and raw flesh. It would take at least two weeks or more for it to heal properly. Only kids who experience this type of punishment can identify with me. Getting the *banan* a second time, before your ass has healed up, is like scalding your hand in boiling water and, while the blisters break and your hand is still raw, scalding your hand again.

None of the kids could remember anyone getting the *banan* twice in one week. The kids who ran away got it twice; once before they went into the *cachot* and eight days later when they got out.

Eighty percent of the time the *banan* was only given to a kid if he ran away, or for more serious offences. I had received it twice in five days, although I had only received six strokes on each occasion. I could see and feel the results of this punishment, but what I could not see was how it affected me mentally, I just know that it did.

Determined to do everything possible to avoid getting it again, I stayed away from the other kids and started reading books. I had been somewhat of a loner before, but now I retreated into my shell and did not let anyone penetrate. Frère Faustin heard that I had been beaten again and tried to help me, but I asked him please not to say or do anything. One of the kids who was working for him in the change room was getting out, and I was chosen to replace him. This was the best thing that could have happened to me. I really loved this job. It was the first time that I was given some responsibility making bundles of shirts and pants for new kids coming in, and I loved it. But the most important thing of all was that I had no fear once I entered the change room. Frère Faustin never gave anyone the strap; he didn't believe in it. He replaced the strap with love and kindness, and, believe me, that was the greatest medicine a kid could get.

Another benefit was that I did not have to go to school anymore and suffer from not being able to understand the lessons. My life became a lot better. I couldn't wait to get to work in the morning, and I tried so hard to do everything right that when Brother Faustin said that I had done a good job, it was music to my ears. He rewarded me with little snacks. One day it was bread and jam, on another it was peanut butter or some kind of meat. He always seemed to have something for me.

This beautiful little man gave me something else that I will treasure all my life, and I pray to God that I can pass it on. He gave me LOVE. This I have come to know today as the most valuable gift that one person can give to another. And as a bewildered, crazy, mixed-up kid who had known nothing but the love of his Mother, this beautiful experience gets more precious as time goes by.

That lesson couldn't erase all the others I had learned, though. The scars on my ass healed, but the hatred in my heart seemed to grow for Brother Laurin. I fell asleep at night dreaming about my revenge. I had a lot of admiration at the time for a notorious hood called Machine Gun Kelly, and I wanted to be just like him. I planned on getting out and making some good scores, buying a machine gun, and making Brother Laurin suffer by shooting him in the feet, then his legs, and then making him suffer like hell before I killed him. I was obsessed with hate for him; a hate I was to carry for a long time.

I have tried to repair the damage of my past, and I have been successful in many areas; however, when a child has been abused physically, mentally, and sexually, you may never be able to dig deep enough to understand or repair the problems. Even so, I know that we must keep trying. I have come to believe and accept that the teachers at this reform school were more toxic than the kids they taught.

CHAPTER THREE

FREEDOM

S pring arrived. I had been at reform school for seven months and I yearned to be free. All I could think of was getting out. I started planning an escape. The reform school was in east-end Montreal in a small suburb called Tetraultville, and most of the kids who tried to escape got caught before they reached the city. Everybody around there knew the clothes the inmates wore, and so if they spotted some kid wearing these clothes they called the police, which resulted in the escapees being picked up within an hour or two.

The brothers always made the inmates stand in line in the big play hall while they took the runaways into the washrooms to give them the *banan*. They must have thought that this served as a deterrent, since we always heard the agonizing screams and cries for help.

You may ask why the kids didn't complain to their parents, and why the parents didn't notify the authorities. I now know that the complaints fell on deaf ears. The Catholic Church was all-powerful in the province of Quebec at that time and any complaints against the priesthood or a religious order were ignored. As far as the government was concerned they could do no wrong.

Most people can't imagine what it's like to live in constant fear. Although I was well-acquainted with fear before I arrived there, it was not a steady diet. In that place I lived with fear night and day. Some of the kids who ran away and were subsequently given the *banan* and then thrown in the *cachot*, came out acting strange and soon were sent to the mad-house half a mile down the road, which was called St. Jean de Dieu. A few never came back, but I guess that with all the big families in those days, one kid here or there wasn't missed. Most of the kids were terrified that they might be sent there.

I planned my escape well. Each dorm had a night watchman on duty from nine P.M. until six A.M. I watched one old guy for many nights and found that he had a routine. He went for coffee or tea about one A.M. That took him about ten minutes, and at about two A.M. he went to the can and sat for twenty minutes to half an hour reading his paper. I had found some clothes in the change room that were darker in colour than our uniform, and had hidden them under my mattress a week before. I decided that the best time to sneak out was two A.M. when the watchman went to the can. Leaving at two A.M. also gave me three or four hours of darkness.

The night before I tried my escape, three other kids tried it and headed for the trees about one hundred yards behind the reformatory. Mr. Roberge, the man in charge of going after the runaways, caught them within a couple of hours. This almost discouraged me from trying. I'll never forget how scared I was that night, and how hard it was to make my final decision. Another thing I had to worry about was my bad case of bronchitis—I never knew when I might have an attack of coughing. I guess this was a result of sleeping under verandas and getting wet too often.

Since my Mom kept telling me at each visit that if I was a good boy and obeyed the rules she could get me out on parole, I knew that if I ran away I would eliminate my chances for parole. I dreaded the thought of my punishment if I was caught, but I also kept thinking about how wonderful it would be to see my Mother and family and friends and to be free. I had been reading a lot of books by Zane Gray, and I would lose myself in those adventure stories. I thought that if I went back and found those wonderful hobos that I knew, I could travel with them and be happy again.

Finally, the magic moment came and I decided to go for broke. I saw the watchman go into the can, he was no sooner in there than I quietly got out of bed and collected my clothes from under the mattress. The brother in charge of the small kids' section slept in a room by the door at the front of the dormitory. I hoped that none of the other kids would see me, and that if they did they would just think I was going to the washroom. Carrying my clothes and my boots to the front of the room, I passed the washroom and the door where the brother slept and slipped out through the front doors of the dormitory. I stood for a moment listening to the sounds, hoping that none of the other kids had noticed me leaving and then crept down the stairs to the second floor. This was the floor where all the classrooms and the chapel were.

I was scared. The thought crossed my mind that I could turn back without anyone being the wiser, and go back to my bed before the watchman came out of the washroom but the thought of being free won out so I slipped into a classroom, put my clothes on carrying my boots so as not to make any noise, and proceeded down to the first floor where the big play-rooms were. I knew that all the doors and windows were locked on this floor, but I had heard by the grapevine that if I could get through the main dining-room in the centre of the building and go to the bakery, I would find a large window with its metal screen broken, and thus easy to open.

Mr. Roberge, the man with the dogs, was about six-foot-five and slim. At this time of the night he would be in the city looking for kids who had already escaped, but his assistant would be making the rounds and I did not want to bump into him. The staff used two big boys, both inmates, to help them find escapees.

I finally got to the refectory and crawled between the tables. This was the room that always had the most traffic. It was in the centre of an enormous building and so I had to be careful. There were doors leading to every part of the building.

As I started crawling between the tables towards the front of the building I stopped dead in my tracks. I could hear faint footsteps and, as I listened they got louder. Many things ran through my mind—some kids may have seen me leave the dormitory and squealed; the watchman may have made his rounds and noticed my empty bed. But as the footsteps came closer and went past me I realized that it was one of the brothers wearing slippers and probably heading for bed.

Well, I finally reached the other end of the refectory and located the door that led to the bakery and the kitchen. It was a swinging door, and as I went through it I saw lights on in the kitchen at the end of the corridor. As I got closer to the bakery I heard voices coming from the kitchen, and one of the voices was unmistakable; once you heard that voice you never forgot it. It was Brother Laurin. I began trembling and I hurried back down the corridor.

My first thought was to rush up to the dormitory and back to my bed where it was safe, but then my trembling subsided a little and I decided to head towards the front door. There were offices there with no screens on their windows, so I thought I'd slip through the first door and crawl past the information counter. There was always someone at the front office, which was right behind the information counter, so I crept along the dark corridor and started trying doors. I got more discouraged at each door, and was soon back at the information counter. They were all locked.

By this time I was really scared and getting desperate. I had to cross the main lobby to get to the corridor on the other side, where the brother would see me if he happened to be looking out the office window. I could hear a radio playing soft music, and it seemed as though I had left the dormitory hours ago.

It was not going the way I planned, and I was beginning to panic. I was thinking of that pig Laurin, and how happy he would be to give me the *banan*. At least this time I would know it was deserved. I quietly crept across the lobby to a corridor on the west side of the building. This was the side where the dogs were kept, and although they were not that vicious, they were well-trained. If they jumped you they held you in their teeth and they would only bite you if you tried to break away. They were yet another obstacle that I had to think about. I went down to the far end of this corridor and proceeded to try the doors again. As I got closer to the lobby and tried the last door I became more discouraged. I was so full of fear by this time that I was actually sick, a feeling I had experienced before when I was waiting outside the washroom for thc *banan*. I decided to retrace my steps and go back down the corridor.

Maybe I should have pushed harder on the doors as I turned the knobs. There were a couple of doormats—maybe there was a key under one of them, but after a lot of wishful thinking and looking over my situation again, my pulse began to quicken as I noticed for the first time that above each door there was a transom. Two or three of these were half-open. I weighed approximately one hundred pounds, and I was not sure whether I could get through the transom or not, but it gave me some hope, and that was better than just standing there.

I picked an office near the end of the corridor and started climbing the wall. I have often heard the expression to "climb the walls," but I would not have thought it very funny that night. I managed somehow to get up on the doorknob. I lost my balance and fell back down on the floor. I prayed that nobody heard me fall. After much effort I succeeded in getting back on the doorknob, hoping that this time I wasn't going to be denied a chance for my freedom.

I was so anxious to get out of there by this time that I went through the transom head first instead of feet first and soon found out that it was not built to support kids of my weight. The window came smashing to the floor, breaking into a hundred pieces and I landed on my head and shoulders. Even though I was dazed, I made a dash for the two windows that led to the outside. I tried to open them but they were either stuck or I wasn't strong enough. I guess they had not been open all winter, and needed a screwdriver or something similar to get them open. I was panic-stricken by now; all I wanted to do was get the hell out of there so I grabbed the first thing I saw—an old typewriter—and threw it through the window and followed right behind it. If you think the transom made a loud noise, this sounded like an explosion. As I hit the ground I just ran and ran, hoping to put as much distance as I could between me and the school.

When I had to stop for a rest, I realized that I was running away from the city instead of towards it. I later learned that this was probably the only reason that I did not get picked up that night. I rested in an old shed behind someone's home, and reviewed my situation. I noticed that one foot was quite wet, so I found a rag and tried to dry it. I sure regretted leaving my boots behind. I had placed them by the door before going through the transom, with the idea of unlocking the door when I got in and grabbing my boots, but everything had happened so fast that I had had no time to stop. As I tried to dry my foot I realized that my sock was wet with blood, and that I must have cut my foot while falling through the window. I wrapped my foot with the rag and started looking for well-stocked clotheslines. Within the hour I had found socks, a shirt and a sweater.

I headed toward the river, about a mile away. I wanted to wash my foot and kill some time until there was more traffic on the roads. I had pulled the sweater on and I was anxious to change my socks and shirt. By the time I got to the river I had scored a quart of milk, something I had not tasted for seven months. The only drink we got at the horror factory was black tea—morning, noon and night—with every meal, so I came to appreciate milk by the time I got out of there. I sat on the river bank washing my feet, watching the ships heading into the harbour and listening to the beautiful sounds of their fog horns. It felt so good to be alive and free.

I guess nobody appreciates freedom as much as those who have been deprived of it. As for fear, I am sure that all people live with a certain amount of fear, and that this can become a burden. I was not entirely free of fear on this beautiful morning but I had left the river bank and headed for one of the main arteries, hoping to jump on the back of a truck to get into the city. In those days most trucks were not closed in as they are today, and I had become adept at hopping them. I would hop on, search for something of value, fill my shirt or jacket, and hop off without the driver being aware of what was happening. But this particular morning I was so embarrassed about being barefoot that I just wanted to get back to my district so that I could get some shoes. It wasn't too long before I was on a truck going west, and with every mile closer to home I grew more excited.

I finally arrived back in my neighbourhood, found some of the guys in my old gang and got a hero's welcome. I phoned my sister Mary later that day and she got in touch with Mom. We all met that night at Mary's, and although my Mom was sorry that I had run away she was very happy to see me, and I her. We decided that I should stay with Mary that night, although I knew that her husband didn't like the idea. I was glad to leave early the next day and headed for the Old Mill, where I was hoping to meet some of my old friends, the hobos, who I was quite sure would help me.

I was very disappointed to find only two hobos there. They told me that the heat was on and that because of so many thefts from the railroad cars the police had cleaned out the Old Mill and other places where the hobos congregated. I thought this was unfair because I knew that the majority of hobos I had met were decent, law-abiding people who would never break into a freight car. The extent of their crimes was to steal rides on the railway and occasionally steal vegetables from someone's garden. They were just guys out of work who thought that the grass might be greener at the next stop.

In retrospect, I should have known that the Old Mill could never have been the same. When I first discovered the Old Mill, I really needed it— there was good companionship, laughter, song and occasionally tears. It was a home away from home and, although I went back at different times trying to recapture that atmosphere, it was not to be.

I got back with my gang and started to appreciate being able to do anything I wanted. I could not see much of my Mom at this time because I knew the authorities would be around home trying to pick me up and return me to the reform school. They usually came at night, hoping to catch me in bed, so the only time I could go near the house was in the daytime when Mom was at work. I really missed her. I was only eleven years old at this time and I could not stay at home or go back to school.

I lived the best way that I could, always with fear of getting caught and being sent back to the École de Réforme. I was sleeping in boxcars, in sheds—anywhere I could.

I came close to getting caught on at least two occasions. One of them was when the cops stopped and asked me to come over to their car. They wanted to talk to me but I ran like hell. Another time, Roberge, the cop from the reform school, came calling in the daytime. He was at the front door, and I knew someone else would be at the back door so I went down in the cellar and hid. He was about to come down and look but when Cy told him that it was full of rats he changed his mind. Since they were coming by every day or two looking for me I did not go near my home often.

There are a few things about this time that stand out in my mind. Among them are the memories of the suffering and heartaches that I caused my Mom. If I could turn back the pages of time, I would return more of the love that she so freely gave to me. Another thing that I remember learning is how much better people treated me if I had money. My status in our community grew at this time and, although I was only eleven years of age, I had friends of all ages. I was later to learn from many bitter experiences that money can be a great attraction, especially to those without any.

I will always remember my first big score. I must have been twelve years old by this time, and was always on the lookout for something to steal.

I had begun stealing out of cars because people sometimes left valuable items in their cars. On one occasion, I was walking down one of the main streets in our neighbourhood when I saw a nice convertible, with a big dog sitting on the front seat. I love dogs, but more importantly, I spotted a woman's purse on the seat and noticed that the car window was open about three inches. This was an opportunity that I couldn't pass up—here was a beautiful leather purse and there was sure to be a lot of money in it.

I had to act fast so I sidled up to the car, wishing I had a bone for the dog. The dog was barking viciously but I had to have that purse. I had dreamed of a situation like this, so I couldn't let this one get away. I told the dog that he was a good dog, that I loved him and I stuck my hand through the window. When I patted him on the head, he didn't attempt to bite me, so I patted him down lower down on his body with the thought of getting closer to the window knob so that I could open the window a little more and get the purse out. I reached my objective, grabbed the purse and headed for the nearest lane. I am sure I did the four-minute mile that night.

When I opened the purse, I became really scared because in it was more money than I had ever seen in my life. There was over two hundred dollars in the purse and to me it seemed like a million. Sure that every cop in the city was now looking for me, I went home that night and hid the money, trying to think of what to do with it. I could not tell my Mom because she was so honest that she would have taken it to the police.

I had to tell someone about it though so the next day I went to see my sister Mary, who lived on the next street. My sister took me downtown and bought me new clothes. I took my sister Theresa, brother Bob, and some of my friends to a big restaurant and we ordered everything we could eat. That was the best day of my life until then. I guess I was "King for a Day." I eventually did get picked up by the police, and was questioned about the purse and where I got the money for the new clothes. In my district, the only time a kid got dressed up was when he died.

Only someone who has gone through the Great Depression, been hungry, and awakened shivering in the night because there was no coal or wood to heat the house can understand the value of a dollar. I can well remember walking up and down the railroad tracks searching for lumps of coal to keep our stove going on winter nights.

One day I noticed my brother Cy counting change on the bed. He was my oldest brother, the one with an amputated leg, and he gave me a couple of cents. I asked him how he had come up with the money. He showed me a postcard with big print on one side that said, "No Bread Today." On the other side it read, "Dear Householder: I have tried every means of obtaining an artificial limb without success. I am therefore obliged to appeal directly to the public. A leg would put me on an equal basis with other men and aid me in getting employment. I lost my leg playing amateur hockey. Anything you can spare will be greatly appreciated." It was signed "Cyril Maloney."

In those days nearly everyone had their bread and milk delivered to their door, and you would often see notes in the window telling the milkman or bread man "No Milk" or "No Bread." Well, Cy had a lot of these cards printed up, and he walked down the street sticking them into people's mail slots. The next day he returned and asked the people if they would like to keep the card and donate something toward him getting a leg.

He asked me to help him put out the cards and

I was glad to help. Depending on how much he made, he would give me ten or fifteen cents. Some days when he did really well I got a quarter. I loved going to the movies, and there were two theatres in our neighbourhood where we could see three pictures for a dime. For a nickel I could either get a bag of stale cakes and buns or a good-sized bag of candies. I loved gangster movies and my favourite actors were James Cagney, George Raft, and Edward G. Robinson. I fantasized a great deal in those days; I could not grow up fast enough to become a gangster.

One day as I was distributing the cards I met a man coming out of a house as I was putting the card in the mail slot. He read the card and looked at my legs. I told him my brother was sick and I was trying to help him. He handed me a dime. This, I think, was the start of my career as a con artist. I thought, "Why can't I just show them the card, tell them my brother is sick, and then collect the money for myself?"

There were two upper-class districts not too far from our neighbourhood. One was the town of Mount Royal and the other was Hampstead. My brother, being an adult, was not allowed to solicit in these districts so I decided to try my luck out there. I was amazed at how easy it was, and it wasn't long before I was collecting more money than my brother, and he never knew!

People would come to the door, I would hand them the card, they would look at my legs, I would tell them that my brother was the one who had one leg and that he was at home in bed with consumption or cancer and that he had saved half the cost of the leg and I was trying to help him get the balance. I realized at this time that the sadder the story the more money they gave, so I became an expert at delivering sad stories. I was forever being asked where I was getting the money from but I never told anyone, not even my own family.

I must have been quite good at my new line of work because at the restaurant where I hung around I was getting a lot of attention. There was always someone who had something important to talk to me about. After each talk I generally had less money in my pocket. I later learned how vulnerable a con artist is to another con. Little did I know at the time that I was becoming a con artist.

Here is an example that taught me a good lesson. I walked into Mary's restaurant one night and, although I was only eleven years of age, I appreciated a good-looking woman. Well, this gorgeous doll walked over to me and introduced herself. Helen started talking, and during the conversation she asked me if I liked rabbits. Well, I am quite sure I had never been close to a rabbit. I told her that I loved dogs and cats but did not know anything about rabbits, so she laid a story on me.

She told me that if I loved dogs and cats I would go crazy over rabbits. She said they were much smarter than dogs, were cleaner than any cat, and added that the rabbit she had at home was so smart and clean that she had taught it to use the toilet. She left the bathroom door open at night so that the rabbit could come and go. It was black and white and nice and furry.

But then Helen told me that she was brokenhearted because she was moving in with her sister, who couldn't stand rabbits. Helen was going to have to sell her beautiful rabbit, but not to just anybody. She was looking for that special person, someone who was kind, and who would love her rabbit as she did. She told me that as soon as she saw me she was sure (woman's intuition) that I was the one who would look after and love her rabbit.

By the time she finished laying this story on me, I would have given her everything I owned for that rabbit. Thank God she only asked for two dollars. I gave her the two dollars and she said that she lived in Rosemount, which was at the other end of town. It was wintertime and it must have been ten or fifteen degrees below zero. We jumped onto a streetcar and warmed ourselves around the pot-bellied stove in the centre of the car.

We finally got there, and I remember how dark and cold it was. We walked down a street and she told me that she did not want her mom and dad to know that she was selling her rabbit. She asked if I would mind waiting in the shed behind the house. I told her I wouldn't mind. I nearly froze to death that night, until finally I rang the front doorbell. No one there had ever heard of Helen or her rabbit! I believe that was one of the best deals I ever made. For two dollars I learned a valuable lesson, and I am sure it saved me a lot of money in my life and made me less gullible. I always wondered what happened to Helen. Our paths never crossed again, and wherever she is I hope she is doing well.

I can't remember how long I remained free. It must have been six or seven months and I guess I got careless. My father left town again and I got together with my brother Cy who talked me into coming home. He told me that Mom would love to see me and that we would have a good time. I really missed Mom and, against my better judgment, I went home. It was to be my last night of freedom.

As I look back, I can never forget the look of pain and the tears that ran down my Mother's beautiful face as I was dragged screaming out of the house by the police and Mr. Roberge from the reform school. There was nothing anyone could do.

I remember thinking of a couple of movies I had seen about Boy's Town in the United States. It was run by Father Flanagan who treated his boys with love and understanding. I was obviously born in the wrong place at the wrong time.

CHAPTER FOUR

RETURN TO REFORM SCHOOL

I f I thought it was bad the first time, they would show me how bad it could really get. They pulled out all the stops. I got the *banan* and was thrown in the *cachot*. I won't even try to explain my feelings in there. I am so full of hate when I remember that hellhole of a school, that even now I cannot help but feel bitter and depressed and pray to God that my tormentors received their just desserts. When I got out of the *cachot* I got the *banan* again, then the *carabole*. Now that I was a marked man (no hair on my head) they could be as mean as they wanted, since I was considered incorrigible.

I decided to apply myself and learn my lessons well. The first lesson was cruelty. I learned that there are so many ways to be cruel, such as walking up behind someone and kicking them, or

71

beating someone with a strap, or putting a small English kid—a *maudit bloke*—in the ring with a big French kid who was taller, heavier, older, and then watching and applauding as the English kid was beaten to a pulp.

There is also mental cruelty, which is even worse. Visits are cut off for three months if you run away. By the third month you are really looking forward to a visit. Your Mom writes and tells you she is bringing your brother and two of your sisters. You are really excited, and when the great day arrives the paper comes through with your name on it, your family is in the visiting room, your excitement increases, but at the very last moment you are told that your visiting privileges have been taken away. You ask why, and you are told you know why. You try to argue or fight for your rights. You are told to stand by the washroom door. You end up getting the strap or *banan*. Instead of the great day you looked forward to, you have had a very lousy day and you learned another very important lesson—HATE.

Oh, how I learned to hate! I survived on hate. What an intense hatred I had for that place and those Christian brothers and their God! What a bunch of hypocrites.

All the kids seemed to respect me more since

my escape. I guess they thought that I had planned to break out that way. I never let them know that the only reason I crashed out was that I was so scared after falling through the transom that I had to keep on going. I heard or read years later that the louder the man, the more scared he is. This I could relate to. All I could think of after my ass healed up was how to escape again. This time I would go out west, so far away that they would never find me, but first, I had to wait for my hair to grow back.

Frère Faustin was still my best friend through all of this time. I can remember so well the times when, after taking a beating or feeling discouraged or depressed, Frère Faustin would show up with an apple, an orange, or some candy and give me some kind words of encouragement. He had a knack of always being near and knowing what to say to make a kid feel better. I think of Frère Faustin when I hear the saying, "There is none so tall as the one who will bend over to help a little kid," or when I hear that beautiful Irish song, *Sure a Little Bit of Heaven Fell from Out the Sky One Day.*

I later became aware that what he really gave me was love. I could not recognize it at the time. I could not even understand it. The only love I had ever known was my Mother's love, and poor Mom was so terribly busy that she could not give us kids as much love as she wanted to.

Frère Faustin soon got me back working in the change room. He had given my job to someone else when I had run away, but the kid who replaced me had only a couple of months to go on his sentence, and so when he was released I was overjoyed to get my old job back. It was like coming into a nice warm living room from a bad winter storm. I spent my time working and reading, and soon had another year in.

Christmas would soon arrive. I had already spent one Christmas in the reform school and I was dying to go home for this Christmas. A lot of kids were getting out for the day, some on Christmas Day and some on New Year's Day, but I soon found out that I was not to be one of them. I got quite bitter because I thought I had been good enough to deserve a break. I started thinking of running away again, and got my chance two days before Christmas.

Every year the school had a Christmas concert that everyone attended. This was the big event of the year. It was held in the big dining hall and the priest and brothers invited guests from outside. I planned to leave about five or ten minutes after the start of the concert. I put on an extra set of underwear that day because it was bitterly cold outside. I scored some clothes, a jacket and sweater, from the change room and put these in my locker, planning on picking them up before I left.

At first, everything went as I had planned. I got out the back door into the big play yard and climbed the fence. I had a choice of heading for the trees and taking the long way around, which would be much safer, or heading straight for the main road. I guess that because it was so cold I got excited, and took the shortcut—the easier, softer way. I was to learn later in life to beware of shortcuts.

Roberge, the security man, and his dog spotted me and there was no way I could outrun them. Before the concert was over, I was back in the *cachot*, to spend the worst Christmas of my life. The morning of Christmas Eve I got the *banan*, and Brother Laurin got his Christmas present early. He was actually joking while giving it to me. Oh, how I hated that bastard! I spent my time in the *cachot* fantasizing about how I was going to kill him. I thought of all kinds of different ways of making the Pig suffer before I cut his throat.

I hardly slept on Christmas Eve, and when I did, it was only for a few minutes at a time. My ass was bleeding and was so painful that I had to sleep on my stomach, or try to. I dreamed of the kids at home and how lucky they were. Mom always had a Christmas tree and we always got Christmas baskets from welfare or the Lions Club. Some well-off woman for whom Mom worked would put our name on their church's list for a basket or box.

How we would cheer and clap and holler! Our names wouldn't be on the gifts, but they would be marked for a seven-year-old girl, or for an eight-year-old boy, and these were always the best presents we got. They were hand-me-downs from rich kids, such as roller skates, a kid's coaster, and games, but we really appreciated and treasured these beautiful gifts and I know how happy it made my beautiful Mom to see us cheerful at Christmas time. I thank God for the wonderful people who took the time to pack the baskets, and donate the food and gifts that made our Christmases so very happy.

All these thoughts made me very sad. I was relieved to hear the kids getting up that morning wishing each other a *Joyeux Noel*, and looking forward to their breakfast of buns and cocoa. After the kids left the dormitory, I was sorry that I could not be with them, and I started to regret my actions of the night before. Why didn't I take to the trees. Why couldn't I have waited until after Christmas—why, why, why …?

My thoughts were interrupted by a loud noise that I recognized as the food wagon coming through the doors of the dormitory. I wondered if we would get bread and water, or buns and cocoa like the rest of the kids. I soon found out that there was only one other kid locked up, and I could hear the brothers telling him to go and wash up—he was getting out because he only had one day left to serve; he would see the Brother Superior the next morning. My hopes started to rise because I thought they might let me out too, but that was too much to hope for.

They opened my door, gave me a bun and a cup of cocoa and left. Whenever I hear that song, *Little Things Mean a Lot,* I think of that Christmas morning when a bun and a cup of cocoa meant so very much.

I got out of the *cachot* on New Year's Eve and took my beating from Laurin; then I went and joined the other kids. This New Year's Eve was a lucky day for me. First of all, Frère Faustin was on duty. That cheered me up because my big worry while in the hole was that someone else would get my job in the change room. But Frère Faustin said that because they were not terribly busy during

Christmas and New Year's, he did not get anyone to take my place. Imagine how happy this made me feel!

That afternoon Frère Faustin brought me a nice lunch in a paper bag: a big meat sandwich, cookies, apple, candies, dates and other goodies. He sure could raise my morale. He gave me hope, encouragement, love and friendship. He was a very quiet man, and years later, whenever I heard the phrase, "A good example is worth a thousand words," I thought of Frère Faustin.

I was determined this time to listen to him and do what he told me, to accept the things I could not change, and to try to make the best of it. His philosophy was to forget about the mistakes made yesterday and to stop worrying about tomorrow. He recommended just doing the best I could today, and he promised that everything would be much better. Once I decided to do what Frère Faustin suggested, things really did get much better. I got the strap occasionally during the next few months and I still had to box whether I wanted to or not, but I had only one serious run-in with Laurin.

I loved skating. The kids were allowed to roller skate in a circle around the big playroom between the tables, which were all around the room, and the lockers, which were up against the wall, and I had borrowed a pair of skates from one of the kids. I was having a lot of fun until one of the kids decided to get something out of his locker. He ran out from behind a beam and I could not avoid hitting him. We were both hurt pretty badly. I hurt my ankle and got a bump on the head and he got banged up too.

It was definitely an accident, but the great Frère Laurin was in charge that day and as usual he made it into a criminal offence—I was going too fast, I was not watching where I was going …. He was going to teach me a lesson, so he sent me over to the washroom to wait for him. I knew what that meant. Luckily, one of the kids I worked with in the change room saw the accident and went up and told Frère Faustin the truth about what had happened.

The kids had returned to their classes or their work and I was standing by the washroom waiting for the *banan*. Suddenly the door flew open and in rushed a very angry Frère Faustin. He walked right over to where I was standing and asked me if I was hurt. I showed him the bump on my head and my swollen ankle. He put his arm around my shoulder and took me over to a table and sat me down. He then turned around to where the other two brothers were and he said, "Laurin, I am taking this kid to the infirmary and I don't want you to ever lay a hand on him again."

When Laurin said that I was not going to leave the room, Frère Faustin took off his Roman collar and his big rosary and, advancing on Laurin said, "Laurin, I call you a coward and a bully, a disgrace to the habit you wear." Sticking his finger in his face he said, "You are a BIG IGNORANT FOOL. If you have any guts at all, show me them!" He pushed the Pig up against the wall and continued, "Show me how you beat the kids! Try beating me."

The Pig was certainly not accustomed to this kind of treatment. Laurin weighed approximately two hundred and fifty pounds, whereas Faustin weighed about one hundred and thirty-five. The other brother and I were amazed to hear that big hulk whimpering like a child and scared out of his wits. I will never forget the sight. I learned a few good lessons that day: "Don't judge a man by his size," "Every dog has his day," and "There is justice after all."

If I hero-worshipped Frère Faustin before, now I idolized him. I followed him around like a little puppy. I was to learn much later in life that what I so admired in this man was that he had Class, with a capital C. Few men are born with it. Others take a lifetime to acquire it. He was the first man that I had gotten to know well that I could really respect and love, although at the time I was so full of hate, I did not know what respect or love was. I did what I was told by Frère Faustin and, sure enough, good things started happening.

For one thing, word had gotten around about Faustin going after the Pig and the kids and the brothers now held him in contempt. He never gave me the *banan* after that. He stayed away from me, and I from him, and what a relief it was. It was now the end of April, and since Christmas I had tried hard to do what was right. Frère Faustin said that I would be getting out for a day in May if I did not do anything bad. Realizing how important a day out of there would be, I was careful not to screw it up.

The great day finally arrived; I think it was the fifteenth of May. My Mom arrived early in the morning to pick me up and it was the greatest day of my life up until then. I had been in school for about nineteen months, where it was always dark and dreary. This beautiful sunny May day was like coming back from the dead. I got home, ate a good breakfast, then I went out to visit my old friends, but as it became closer to the time of my return, I knew I couldn't go through with it. I wanted to put as many miles between me and that reform school as I could.

I had heard from some of my friends that the O'Haras, a family down the street from us, had moved to Hamilton, Ontario. David O'Hara was a good friend of mine and his sister, Mary, who was about fifteen, was a beautiful little blonde whom I liked a lot. Hamilton was about four hundred miles from Montreal, and so I thought I would be safe there—as long as I could get there. I got the O'Hara's address from friends and asked my Mom for bus fare. My Mom felt bad about my running away again, but she knew I would hitchhike if I didn't get the money, so she bought me a bus ticket for Hamilton. I arrived the next morning and went looking for the O'Haras.

They lived down the street from a big Westinghouse plant and were not hard to find. They were glad to see me and they told me how much better off they were since they moved there. The old man had gotten a job at the Westinghouse plant, Dave was working at a soda fountain in a drugstore after school and he thought it would be easy for me to find a job. I remember being so happy and thinking that maybe Mr. and Mrs. O'Hara would adopt me, and that I could live with them and never have to go back to the reform school.

After a week or so of searching the Hamilton

classified section every day for a job, I finally found one in a bakery, washing pots and pans. The year was 1939, and I was twelve years old. My pay was ten cents an hour and the hours I worked were irregular. Some days I worked eight hours, other days ten or twelve hours; six days a week. It averaged out to about sixty hours a week, and my week's pay was around six dollars. I only paid four dollars for my room and board, so the balance of two dollars was a lot of spending money. I felt like a big shot.

Another thing I had going for me was that Dave was working in a big drug store. I'd give him a one-dollar bill and he'd give me change for a five or a ten. I don't remember whose idea that was, but it was profitable until we got too greedy and the boss found out. David was fired and his folks blamed me. They were right. I think I started to become aware that trouble seemed to follow me wherever I went—I was a misfit.

This had been a great opportunity for me to have a new beginning and to start a new life but I'd blown it. When I was asked to leave the O'Hara's home I started looking for a room and on my payday I moved out into a basement room in a slum neighbourhood for two dollars a week.

Some people might call it puppy love, but I

had fallen head over heels in love with Mary O'Hara and was heartbroken when I had to leave. I wanted so much to belong somewhere. This taste of normal living with a family created in me a great hunger for a stable, happy life. It took me many years to find a life, and many more to learn how to live and enjoy it.

I soon fell back into my old habits—stealing from parked cars, shoplifting—until I was arrested and held in the Barton Street Jail in Hamilton, Ontario. They tried to find out where I was from but I certainly wouldn't tell them. They had placed me in solitary confinement when I was arrested, but then I was put into a cell with another guy. I was lonely and began talking too much, and I told him all about myself. I soon learned he was a stoolie and told the cops everything I had told him.

The cops sent a wire to the reform school in Montreal informing them that they had one of their escapees and asking them to send someone to pick me up to take me back. The reform school sent a wire back that made me a very happy boy—they said that I had been a lot of trouble and that if they took me back I would probably run away again. So they did not want any more trouble from me, and since the Hamilton police had me, they could keep me.

Some years later when a psychiatrist asked if I had ever felt abandoned or unwanted, I told him my family didn't want me, the police didn't want me, but my most embarrassing moment came when I found out even the reform school didn't want me. I was the only kid in Montreal who was expelled from a reform school!

I soon passed in front of a judge and was on my way to Toronto to spend an indefinite period in St. John's Industrial Training School. I was surprised that they did not call it a reform school, but I was soon to find many pleasant surprises. One of the first things that I noticed was the absence of fences around the building. It must be easy to run away, I thought. Then, as I was escorted into the building, I saw some other strange things that flabbergasted me. First, there were kids walking around laughing and making jokes, and the brothers-in-charge were doing the same.

I was introduced to the brother-in-charge, who began calling me by my first name. He said, "Earl, you will find the rules written up on the board in the hall. I want you to read them, and if there is anything you don't understand, don't be afraid to ask questions. We will help you in any way we can." I was nervous, sitting there in front of him, but he spoke to me as a friend, and he seemed to know how I felt; even more importantly, he seemed to care.

His name was Brother Kevin Ryan, and up until then nobody in authority—not my father, the judges, the authorities at the reform school, the police—had ever sat down and talked to me like this man, except Frère Faustin. I was confused when I left his office because of the treatment I got, but what impressed me the most was when he told me that whatever I had done in the past would be forgotten and forgiven and that I could start over with a clean slate. I felt very good and made up my mind to do what was right.

The next big surprise was the food. I can truthfully say that I had never eaten this well in my life. In the morning, instead of the grease and mustard I had been receiving in Montreal, I had a choice of cereal; fried or boiled eggs; bacon, ham or sausage; real butter; and, best of all, milk and coffee to drink. I was astounded at the difference, and had to pinch myself to make sure this was not all a dream. It was like going from Hell to Heaven.

Whereas Frère Faustin had stood out as the exception rather than the rule at the reform school in Montreal, here at St. John's if a boy had a problem, he could talk about it with any brother who was available. Although I did not realize it at the time, the most important change in my day-to-day life was not having to live with the fear of being punished at any moment. I knew that if I were punished I would certainly have done something wrong. This was a great relief, and so I started gaining weight, and my schoolwork began to improve.

We were only a couple of blocks from Lake Ontario, and after school we walked down to the shore to go swimming, then came back and had supper. After supper we went out and played baseball or volleyball or some other sport. The brothers were our coaches and they were really fair. They did their best to teach us the fundamentals of the games we played.

When school was finished in June, we were all taken to a summer camp. We went boating, hiking and swimming. We played touch football and tug-of-war, and at night we sat around the campfire singing songs and taking part in wiener and marshmallow roasts. I thought a lot of my old friends back in Mont St.-Antoine in Montreal, and wished they could be here with me. None of the kids ever sang in Montreal—the most common sound was crying. I can recall only one kid who sang once in a while, and he ended up in the nuthouse.

There was only one thing wrong with my Shangri-La—I was lonesome. I really missed my Mom and family back home. I wrote often and got letters from home, but I yearned to hold my Mother and hug her. I could not keep her out of my thoughts. I guess I needed the love of a Mother, so I began thinking of running away again.

We were in the late fall season and I had been there for about six months. This was football season and I was playing as a running back. My coach was Brother Kevin Ryan, a former football player. I admired him and always wanted to please him by playing my very best. I scored quite a few touchdowns and his praise was music to my ears.

It was late in November when I played my last game. I had the ball, and I only had to get by this Indian kid they called Beaver. Well, I must have forgotten to duck because he gave me a straight-arm and broke my nose. I continued to play, but after the game my nose was quite swollen so they took me to St. Michael's Hospital in downtown Toronto. I was accompanied by a brother and an inmate. I was left in the waiting room while the brother and the other kid went off to find a doctor. I just got up and walked out.

I went to a nearby church and killed some time, hoping they would not look too hard for me.

I left the church about an hour or so later and walked west for a mile or two until I came to some railroad tracks. I had always wanted to ride the freight trains, and I thought, "Here's my chance." I walked along the tracks for a couple of miles until I came to a freight train that was taking on coal or water. I realized then that I did not know much about taking a freight, so I just climbed up the steel ladder on the side of a freight car and lay down on the crosswalk on its roof. Later, I often thought about how dumb that was.

CHAPTER FIVE

RUNNING

I had no idea which direction the freight train was going to take. I wore only a shirt and a pair of pants and it was a frigid November night. The brother had told me to take my coat before I left for the hospital but, as usual, I did not take his advice. The train started off down the tracks. I was holding on to a short iron crossbar that went over the crosswalk and I was taken for a ride I will never forget.

The train went faster and faster into a biting wind, and I became colder and colder until I started getting numb. The only thing I could do was hold on and pray that the train would soon stop. When the train finally stopped in Kingston, Ontario, half the way to Montreal, I was so numb and exhausted that I could not get my hands off the iron bar. I thought at first that they were frozen stiff, but I kept trying because I was afraid that the train would start again. After a few minutes of blowing my breath on them, I got them loose and jumped down from the train.

I headed for the caboose at the back of the train, not caring what they did to me as long as I got warm. I knocked on the door of the caboose and a man opened the door. I told him that I had been to Toronto to find work but could not find any, so I was trying to get back to Montreal. I gave him a real sad story. He could see that my nose was swollen and my teeth were chattering together. I must have been a pathetic sight.

He brought me into the caboose and I headed right for the beautiful potbellied stove and, although it was nearly red hot, I felt like hugging it. I have never appreciated the warmth of a stove as I did that night. He told me that this was an express freight train, that we were in Kingston, and that we would be in Montreal around six o'clock in the morning. He said I could use his bunk and that he would wake me just outside Montreal, where I would have to get off at a place called Turcott Yards. It seemed as if I passed out from exhaustion as soon as I laid down, because the next thing I knew he was shaking me to tell me we were coming into Montreal. He asked me if I had money for the bus and when I said I was broke he gave me a quarter. I will be forever grateful to that wonderful person for the help he gave me.

I headed home and had a great reunion with the family. I was so very happy to see my Mom and she was so surprised to see me. My old man's feelings had not improved by my absence. He was still snarling every time he saw me, so I tried to stay out of his way.

Cy was always telling jokes; I don't think he ever forgot a joke. He could keep us laughing all day when he wanted to. He also was in great demand in all the taverns he frequented in our district. He had a large following that seemed to grow and grow. Although he never did become very fluent in French, he could always tell jokes in French. I was always amazed at how he could laugh at misfortune, although he only had one leg. After an accident with a trolley car, he became quite deaf and had to wear a hearing aid.

One morning I woke up and heard that Cy was gone. He had left Mom a note saying that the cops were hassling him and that, since he did not want to cause her any more trouble, he was going to Vancouver. I know Mom took it very hard. Cy was the firstborn in the family and Mom loved him very much. There was no laughter in our house for quite some time.

About a month or so later, Mom got a letter from Cy in Vancouver telling her that he had arrived there all right and that he had travelled all the way by freight train. He had a nice room with nice people and told her not to worry about him. Mom seemed to get a great lift from that letter and I can remember being very proud of him and telling all my friends of his long trip, over three thousand miles by freight train. I did not realize how much I would miss him.

When Cy left, the laughter left and home got very dull. I guess it was just as well because I only went home when there was nowhere else to go. It was not long after I arrived back in Montreal that I met some of my old friends that I used to steal with. And it wasn't long before I fell in love. Doreen was very pretty, and I figured that I had to steal to make money to take her out. She wouldn't come across for me because she was a virgin; so I ended up going to my first whorehouse. What a great experience.

I had heard where they were, so some other kids and I liked walking past the shuttered windows, looking at the girls. The first time I saw them I knew I had to have them. Whorehouses were legal at the time and the girls were getting a medical check-up once a week. I picked a Sunday morning to go and visit a whorehouse when I knew the old man was dragging the other kids off to church. I will never forget how excited I was, while also being afraid that they would turn me down. I had two dollars in my pocket, plus some loose change. I knew the prices ranged from fifty cents to two dollars. I planned on walking down Burger Street and up de Bouillion, picking out the nicest looking woman.

But when I got there, and bravely walked past the first house and heard the familiar "phsst," "phsst," I nearly fainted. At the second house the same thing happened and I walked in. I am sure I could not have made it to the end of the block. This woman was in her twenties, I guess, and to me at that moment, she looked beautiful. She asked me to get undressed while she went to get a bowl of water, a towel and face cloth. When she came back I was still dressed and scared as hell. I thought of running back out of the house but I was afraid of what I would miss. She was very kind and comforting and helped me undress. She then washed me, and I can assure you that I got my two bucks worth. What I also found out that morning was that this was the greatest feeling I had ever experienced in my life, and that, although I did not realize it at the time, I was hooked. I was addicted to women. I was thirteen.

I was in heat every waking hour. Some say that sex is a problem, but I found it to be the best problem I have ever discovered. It took me to new heights in ecstasy and I'll cherish those experiences and memories till my dying day. I thought it would be great if I could find more problems like this because it relieved me of my fears and frustrations at the time. I did not think this a problem. I thought everyone felt the same way that I did. I later found out that it was an obsession that I could not always control. Of course, not knowing it was a problem, I enjoyed it to the fullest. Someone told me once—I don't remember who—that if you played with yourself too much you would end up in a mental hospital. That scared me for a little while but I soon forgot it.

I recall that around this time I worked for Benny's Meat Market, delivering groceries. One day I delivered an order to a beautiful French woman. She answered the door in a black negligee that was partly open. I could see enough of her to get very excited. She asked me to put the groceries on the kitchen table. What groceries!

Her voice was coming from a room off the

kitchen, so I walked in the direction of her voice. It was coming from the bedroom. She was half-lying and half-sitting on the bed, leaning over the bedside table. Her negligee was partly open and I could see all of her legs and part of her pink panties. I think I went into shock. I could hear her making small talk, asking how long I had been working at Benny's and how I liked the job, and explaining that she was a regular customer. By this time I guess I was panting. She asked me if I would like to sit down beside her on the bed; I was sitting before she had the last word out. She told me how mean her husband was, that he was always leaving her alone, and that she was so lonesome. I said that he must be crazy to leave a beautiful woman like her alone. I then told her how much I would love her if I were her husband. Suddenly she started crying. Not knowing what to do, I started patting her on the head. She rolled over on her side and I continued patting her, but my hands now went down her beautiful flesh. Then I lay down beside her and she turned around and kissed me, telling me that I could take my clothes off if I wanted to.

I can remember how awkward I was, but when I got into bed she was so tender and gentle that I had a climax before I even entered her. I stayed around until I was ready again and this time I did it properly or so she said. Jeannine would call for some groceries every morning after that and I would get so excited when I was given her order to deliver. She taught me so much, but I guess it was too good to last. She suddenly stopped ordering groceries, and a week or so later I found out from a neighbour that she had left her husband and gone back to her folks on the farm. I'm grateful to Jeannine for one of the greatest experiences of my life. It took quite a while to get over Jeannine. I kept comparing girls to her and it was a long time before I met one who could make me forget her.

My job became dull round about then, whereas it had been so exciting before. I had experienced heartaches, but this was a new kind of heartache that I had never felt before, and I believed it was at this time that a song became very popular on the jukeboxes. It was, *They Tried to Tell Us We're too Young*. I also would hear the song, *Oh, How I Miss You Tonight*; and I would go somewhere by myself and feel very sad. I must have been sentimental. Anyway, it was at this time that I started to drink. I would throw a couple of pints of beer in the grocery orders that I was delivering, stash them away and at night after work I would drink and forget my troubles.

The first time I can remember drinking alcohol was when I was about six or seven. My brother Cy would give me a nickel if I would drink a glass of alcohol, which was eighty or ninety proof alcohol. It was a strong drink, and I guess that when I drank it I acted strangely. He got his kicks watching me perform.

Well, now after a few beers I became another person. Sober, I would be shy and reserved but after two or three beers I could talk to the girls and lose all my fear. I went looking for fights with kids older and bigger than myself because I thought at the time that alcohol was the equalizer that would put me on the same level as other kids. I am sure that I became addicted at the age of thirteen, and from then on I could not seem to do anything without a drink.

Shortly after I started drinking, my family moved downtown and I met some new friends at a small restaurant called Pop's Music Box. I now started to steal in earnest. Every night I was out with one or two friends breaking into stores or rolling some poor drunk who may have taken one drink too many. I became adept at strong-arming drunks.

I met a girl by the name of Peggy. She was pretty and about sixteen. She would go into a nightclub and look around until she found a drunk flashing a roll. Then she would strike up a conversation with him and, when he was loaded, she'd phone me and tell me she had a live one. I'd go over to the club and follow them. We usually prearranged the route that she'd take with the drunk, and it was often through McGill College campus or up on the mountain, both of which were close to the downtown clubs. I always carried a length of pipe or at least a pop bottle, just in case I ran into someone I couldn't handle, but ninety percent of the time we got what we wanted without any violence.

I always had to have a few drinks before I could perform these acts; I guess I knew even then that without alcohol I was a scared kid. Not that any of these actions were brave, but with alcohol I could become vicious, cruel and sadistic. I soon became known to the police. They started picking me up for questioning, holding me two or three days and then letting me go. I took a few good beatings at first, but after a while they eased up on trying to beat a confession out of me.

In one year I had progressed from breaking and entering to robbery with violence, and now I was running with a hold-up gang. There was George, Joey, Billy and me. We would walk into a store when there were no customers and stick a gun in the owners' faces. When they handed over the money we grabbed anything we saw of value and ran like hell. We always met at the same place after a hold-up to share our booty. We never got too much, but we thought we were tough guys. We went to all the gangster movies, such as *Public Enemy Number One*, and *High Sierra* with Humphrey Bogart. I recall trying to talk like Bogart, smoking with the cigarette hanging from the side of my mouth and always turning my coat collar up. I could really fantasize.

I have to laugh now when I think of how seriously I played my role, especially when I had a couple of drinks in me. I am sure I actually believed that I was the person I was playing. I also had a great imagination, and I loved the song, *Imagination Is Funny—It Makes a Cloudy Day Sunny,* because I could identify with it.

I would be arrested and held in the trial ward for a month or so, and by the time I got to court I had a story well thought-out. It was always full of lies, but it nearly always worked—I knew that if I believed the story myself the judge would more than likely believe it. It was usually dramatic, well-rehearsed and polished before I appeared in front of the judge. For a long time I gave my lawyers credit for springing me, until one lawyer told me that I did not need him, that the job I did on the judge was a better job than he could have done.

One night, when George and Billy did not show up at Pop's, where we usually met, Joey and I decided to go out alone. We figured we would make more money because there would only be a two-way split. We had been planning on knocking off this grocery store for quite a while. It was on Park Avenue, which was one of the main streets in Montreal, and it had a license to sell beer, which indicated that it would have more money in the cash than other places. We cased the joint pretty well and when we saw that there were no customers in the store, only the owner and his messenger boy, we decided to hit it. All the places we had held up before were quite simple, and there were only a couple of times when we had been chased. This time was a little different.

We walked into the store and pretended to be shoppers. Our plan was to pick up something and take it to the counter, and when the cashier punched the cash I was to pull the gun on him. But just after entering the store, while we were approaching the cashier with a couple of articles, two men came in. I pretended we had forgotten something and went back to get it. By the time the two men left we had become a little unnerved and I think the owner suspected something. We should have walked out, but we did not have enough money to pay for the articles we had picked up, so I headed for the cashier and pulled out the gun. Then all hell broke loose.

Instead of giving me the money, the cashier started screaming and calling us names. His wife came running from the back of the store, the messenger boy grabbed Joey, and I headed for the front door. I dropped the gun on the way out and the owner picked it up. He yelled at me to stop as he chased me down the street, but I was too scared to stop. He shot at me twice. Thank God there were only two bullets in the gun.

As I was running up the mountain, which was about three blocks from the hold-up scene, I noticed that my right foot and shoe were soaking wet, making a squishing sound as I ran. I thought that I must have stepped in a puddle of water, so imagine my surprise when I sat down and inspected my shoe—it was full of blood. The blood was coming from a hole in my leg. My immediate thought was that I had somehow cut my leg running from the scene, and the sight reminded me of my escape from the reform school years before.

In desperation, I tore the sleeve from my shirt, bandaged up my leg, and headed for home. Lucky for me, Cyril was there, and after I had explained what had happened, he lay me down and cleaned out the wound. Suddenly he let out a holler that shocked me. "There's a bullet in your leg!" he exclaimed, "We're gonna have to get you to a hospital."

How could I have been shot and not have known it? I knew one thing, though—I couldn't go to any hospital because the staff would turn me over to the police. So Cy operated on me. He made me take three Nembutals (a powerful sleeping pill), and I was soon out like a light. He told me later that he got the bullet out with a pair of barber's scissors. I didn't feel a thing. For years afterwards, whenever Cy got drunk, he bragged about the operation from beginning to end.

I was really scared by now, and realizing that they had caught Joey, I wondered if he would stool on me. I was also worried about the gun. The police had taken my fingerprints a couple of times when I was picked up for questioning, and I was worried about them finding my fingerprints on the gun. As I sat there, I began to reflect on the past and I didn't like the picture I saw. I remembered how I felt when I was given five years in the reform school, but this time I knew that if I got caught I would go to the penitentiary—the reform school wouldn't take me back. I had to change my way of living. I had a premonition that I was heading toward disaster. I was so impulsive that once I made the decision to leave town, I couldn't leave fast enough.

I stuffed a small overnight bag with a sweater and a couple of pairs of socks, headed for the highway, and started hitchhiking. I always got a high when I was heading into the unknown, but this time the trip was uneventful and I landed in Toronto tired and hungry. I found an all-night restaurant called Bowle's Lunch, on the corner of Queen Street and Bay, and I soon became acquainted with some local rounders, drifters, boosters, and all types of lost people.

As I sat and looked out the big windows onto the street, I saw the city coming alive and became exhilarated. Everything seemed to be new and different. It wasn't long before the streets were full of people heading for work or going about their business. There seemed to be excitement in the air and I wanted to be a part of it. I think I fell in love with Toronto that morning. That first impression has remained with me to this day.

I left the restaurant that morning with a booster who knew the ropes and took me to a few of the department stores in the area. He was very good at his chosen profession, and it wasn't long before we had enough swag and could take the rest of the day off. We then made the rounds of a couple of hotels and restaurants where he sold the stuff we had stolen for about one third or half of what it was worth. When we met he told me his name was Bryan, but everybody called him Pee Wee. He was well-liked and popular with the people we met and it wasn't long before I was accepted as one of them.

I could not stick to any one thing. I liked variety. I was what is referred to as a "cat burglar." I'd climb on fire escapes, rooftops, ledges—wherever I thought there was something valuable. One day Pee Wee and I were walking down an alley in back of Yonge Street when I asked him to give me a lift up so that I could look into a barred window. It was an exclusive ladies' dress shop, which had a change room just beneath the window. In the change room was a table, and on this table was an expensive-looking purse. I signalled to Pee Wee to help me down and informed him of what I had seen. We decided to look for a wire coat hanger and some string so that we could throw our line down to hook the purse. We found what we needed close by and went back to fish for the purse. We hooked it within a few minutes and we were well rewarded for our efforts. We always wondered how the owner explained to the customer the disappearance of her purse.

We kept falling into situations and opportunities that made life exciting and kept us hopping. I was staying with Pee Wee, and each night we would rehash and reminisce about all our past experiences or what our plans were for the future. Each night we would always seem to end up talking about carnivals and circuses. Pee Wee had been with Conklin Shows the year before. It was the largest carnival in Canada. He said he had a great time and that he was thinking of joining them again that year. I was all for it.

The carnival was planning to hit the road in a couple of weeks from their winter quarters in Brantford, Ontario, and we wanted to be with them. I can truthfully say, for a kid who has survived on the streets and has acquired some street smarts, carnival life is like going to high school where you can really learn the tricks of the trade in conning, swindling and finding the marks or suckers.

Pee Wee introduced me to a lot of people that he already knew. I learned that this year a circus was joining the carnival during the tour. The circus was called Terrel Jacob's Wild Animal Shows. I went to see them right away and they hired me to do general work around the circus, cleaning up the elephant shit, feeding the animals, washing and brushing the elephants and all sorts of odd jobs. I loved every minute of it.

Terrel Jacobs was the owner and lion tamer. I loved watching his and all the other animal acts, the elephants, bears, seals, horses, and dogs. I was in heaven. I pictured the poor kids who were going to school, and thought of myself as one of the luckiest kids in the world. I soon found out, though, this was not all fun, especially when we had to tear down the big top and set it up again in a town just down the road.

There was a lot of hard work involved, but we had help from the elephants. They did most of the heavy work and seemed to know exactly what their jobs were. After lifting the centre pole into place the trainer would shout out commands and before long you could see the big top taking shape like a giant jigsaw puzzle before your eyes. We usually arrived in a town in the early hours of the morning and worked like hell so that everything was ready for the noon opening of the big top.

The excitement seemed to abound as the

crowds began to arrive, and the circus music became louder, and the barkers tried to be heard above the sound of the music and laughter, trying to convince people that their show was the greatest of them all. I have always felt that most people who enter a carnival midway or a circus big top seem to leave their troubles outside and seem to get lost in a world of make-believe. A doctor could not have prescribed better medicine for me at this particular time than joining the world of the carnie and circus people. They were one big happy family, and their motto was, "One for all and all for one." If you were in any trouble with the paying customers, you hollered, "Hey Rube," and your brothers and sisters ran from all directions to help you.

Strangely enough, I enjoyed and felt more at home with this new family than I ever had with my own. I found myself with some free time during the circus acts and began working as a shill. A shill's job is to win prizes at the different concessions and to take them back later. The concessionaires gave me the money to play with and I used this money for hot dogs, hamburgers, and other goodies. I enjoyed this job and got acquainted with the other shills. Every game had one or two shills.

I was working the Panda Bear Game. It had a

roulette wheel that was fixed to take in sixteen dollars for every panda bear that went out. Conklin had this game and a few others and hired people to run them for him. He bought his prizes by the thousands. At that time panda bears were probably a dollar each, so he ended up with a profit of, say, ten dollars each. He became a millionaire.

I realized that every game in the show was fixed. If I had the right connections I could make some extra money. For instance, if I needed a radio or overnight bag, clock, etc., I could play bingo, where they gave out these articles as prizes, and they would let me win the prize I needed. The operator would just pick up my card when I hollered bingo. He would call off the four or five winning numbers and, although they were not on the card I gave him, I would still win. I could never enjoy bingo after this because it was too easy to fix. All the other games were fixed too so that the poor suckers who played them did not stand a chance. I felt really bad when some poor kids put their last dime on a number, and I saw the disappointment on their faces when they lost. It was not all fun at the show.

What we all dreaded the most were the nights when we had to tear down in the rain. We would get all wet, our feet and legs would be covered in mud, and the canvas would soak up the rain, making it so much heavier to roll and lift on to the trucks and trains.

Conklin Shows had a train to move the equipment and the people who worked for the show, and Paddy Conklin had a private car in the back of the train. If I remember correctly, the cars that followed were for the people in order of importance: the people who rented space from him to run their own concessions, juice joint operators, people who ran the shows, others who were in charge of the rides, and on down the line. Then came the dining car, called the "Pie Car," and last, but not least, was the gazooney car. The people in this car were made up of the least important, like the freaks in the freak shows, the roustabouts, and a few mixed-up kids like myself.

One of the other kids was a young girl who everyone called Ballet Lucky. Her real name was Linda Kelly and she worked in the freak show. Her act was quite simple. She would be tied to a large cross with ropes and would stand out on the stage (ballet) in front of the show. Because she was a very attractive blond girl in shorts and halter, people would stop and stare at her while the barker hollered about how she had been a slave in a sheik's harem, and how, because she had superhuman strength, she had broken the chains and ropes that held her and had escaped back to this country. If they would all buy a ticket and come in she would show them how she made her escape.

It was all lies, but the suckers just ate it up and rushed to the ticket booth. Then, as the tent filled up with people, Ballet Lucky would pull her arms from the cross, and the ropes would seem to break and fall from their moorings, but really there were little clips on the ropes that any ten-year-old could have broken. I am reminded of what P. T. Barnum, the American showman, said, "There's a sucker born every minute." When I think of Lucky's rope trick I know that there were all kinds of tricks to relieve the suckers of their money.

In the gazooney car there were all sorts of people pairing up. It had been a sleeping car at one time but it was ready for the scrap heap. There were just so many berths in the car and we slept two to a bunk. Lucky was paired with a black girl from the freak shows, while I was paired with another kid who worked in the circus. Lucky and I had gotten bottom bunks across from each other, and we became close friends. We had a lot in common. She also had run away from home because her father was a drunk and had been assaulting her sexually and physically until she couldn't take it anymore; so she ran away and ended up here like myself. It was not long before I changed bunks with the black girl, and all that summer we had a torrid love affair.

Lucky became aware that she was pregnant and went to see a doctor to confirm it. We made all kinds of plans about getting married and starting a home together, but as the season wore on and eventually came to an end I think we both realized that we were too young to get married and also too young to start a family. So, when the season ended we went to Toronto together and I stayed with Lucky for a few more days. Then she came to the train station and saw me off. As I was saying good-bye to her we both started crying, and she promised to have the baby and put it up for adoption. We both promised that we would be in Brantford the following April to join the shows again, and I believe that when we made these promises we meant them; but I was never to see Lucky again. I hope she has found a good guy, and that her life has turned out as well as mine. I am ashamed for not trying to find her and help her with the baby. I have to live with this.

I returned to Montreal and soon found out that the police were not looking for me, and that poor Joey had been sentenced to two years in

Shawbridge Boy's Farm, which was a nice place for Protestant kids. I had always wished that I could have been sent there, rather than to Mont St.-Antoine, the horror factory.

With my first good score I bought a few presents and went up to visit him. He was really surprised to see me. I thanked him for not stooling on me, left him some money and came back to town. I soon got back with the old gang and got back into the old routine of playing cops and robbers and hanging out at Pop's Music Box. I got to drinking a lot now. My dependency on alcohol was increasing to the extent that I could not do anything without a drink.

With the drinking, I started having more and more blackouts. Friends would tell me some of the things I did the night before and I could not remember doing them. I became fearless when I drank or, I guess I should say, out of my mind. Alcohol took me to many strange places and made me do many strange things. It was like getting on a merry-go-round and not being able to get off. I began taking on guilt feelings and also began carrying a load of fears that I could only get rid of with a drink. At the time, of course, I did not know what was happening to me. I was just a scared, frustrated kid, so I just kept trying to ride out the storm.

I was also introduced to marijuana around this time, more commonly known as grass, and it also had a strange effect on my behaviour. It calmed me down and let me dream in Technicolor; it also increased my capacity for sex. Not that I needed any increase, because I was oversexed to begin with. I could never get enough, but marijuana seemed to make the foreplay and the pleasure last longer. I was uninhibited when using this drug. Now I was hooked on two drugs, alcohol and marijuana, but I did not realize the danger and I did not know where they would lead me, so I just accepted them as part of growing up.

I had to steal more because my new habit was expensive. I recall meeting some kids who were breaking into homes, and they seemed to be doing quite well, so I decided to try housebreaking along with the other capers that I was committing. I soon mastered it. My new partner was a kid named Johnny, and we soon picked up a screwdriver and a piece of celluloid. Housebreakers called them "loids," and you can become adept at opening nearly any door by sticking the loid in between the lock and the panel of the door. We would go in and pick up anything of value and leave the door unlocked when we left so the occupants would think they had left their door unlocked.

After we robbed a house we went downtown to a fence who robbed us by taking our loot for as little as ten percent of the real value. Fences were the ones who made the money. We knew a fence who was also a second-hand furniture dealer, and so when we heard of people who were on vacation, we broke into their house and called him up. He came with a truck and we sold him everything of value in the house. I should have had a guilty conscience because of the things I was doing, but I felt good when I robbed or hurt someone. I am sure this was the result of the lessons I learned at the reform school and at the hands of the cops and my father.

One night as I was walking down the street, a car pulled alongside of me and I was told to get into the back. There were two detectives in the front and two in the back. I was placed in between the two in the back seat and they started searching me. They found a new pen and pencil set, a small flashlight, a set of skeleton keys, a loid, and over a hundred dollars in cash. They knew that I had stolen the money and they threatened to beat me until I told them where each item had come from. I told them I had bought the flashlight and the pen and pencil set, found the keys and the loid, and won the money gambling. They called me a liar and then one of the big bastards reached over, grabbed my left hand and broke my small finger. He told me he was going to break one finger at a time until I told the truth.

I got a bad beating that night and ended up in the interrogation cells at police headquarters. Incidents like this increased my hatred for cops and made me more and more antisocial. I began to enjoy breaking the law. I thought of it as a game played between me and the authorities. The more robberies and thefts I got away with, the worse they looked. Eventually the day came when, if I had a choice between doing something right and doing something wrong, I always chose doing it wrong.

There were two Irish cops in the downtown area who had arrested me on numerous occasions—Officers Brennan and O'Neil. They were always picking me up for something, and they knew that I was responsible for a lot of robberies in their district. They were determined to send me to jail, but time after time I was acquitted, which just made them more determined to get me.

I had a terrific lawyer at this time called Chevalier, and I am sure that a couple of the judges were his cronies. I remember him always remanding my cases until he could get me in front of a certain judge who always threw my case out of court for lack of evidence.

I remember one case where I was certain that Chevalier couldn't win. I had robbed a restaurant and stashed the stolen goods in a tourist room above Pop's Music Box. The place was called "New Moon Rooms." I had filled the drawers of the bureau with cartons of cigarettes and loose cigarette packets and on top of the bureau I had placed a bag of silver coins. I later learned that there were seventy-nine dollars in coins in the bag.

Well, the following night at about midnight I decided to go up to the room for something and I put the key in the lock and opened the door. I flicked on the light and found Brennan and O'Neill sitting on the bed waiting for me. I was surprised, but they were delighted to see me. They said they had known that they would eventually catch me with the goods, and that there was no possible way that I could slip out of this one.

They loaded the stolen goods and me into the car and headed for police headquarters. When we got there they called the owner of the restaurant in to make a positive identification of the stolen goods, which he did. They then told me that it would go a lot easier for me if I signed a confession or made a statement. But all I told them was that somebody was trying to frame me and that I didn't know how the loot got in my room.

A couple of days later, at the preliminary enquiry, the cigarettes and the bag of silver coins were spread over the prosecutor's table. It sure looked like an open-and-shut case until the owner of the restaurant, who was Jewish, got into the witness box and swore on the Bible that the cigarettes and money were positively his and that he could not be mistaken. Out of the corner of my eye I could not help noticing the two grinning detectives.

Then it was Chevalier's turn to cross-examine the witness, and he got the witness to admit that the Bible did not really mean anything to him and that he was not a believer of the Bible. Then Chevalier walked over to the prosecutor's table, took two packets of cigarettes out of his pocket, mixed them in with the other cigarettes and asked the witness to come down and find his cigarettes. After more questioning he got the witness to admit that all the cigarettes were the same, that they just looked like his cigarettes, and that the same was true of the money. Then Chevalier approached the bench, summed up his case and convinced the judge that in no way could the witness positively identify either the cigarettes or the money as being his, and concluding that the case should therefore be dismissed. The judge agreed and dismissed the case.

An oddity of this case is that the prosecutor asked the judge what he should do with the cigarettes and the money. The judge said to return them to me, and so I walked out of the courtroom with a potato bag full of cigarettes and the bag of coins. Chevalier later told me that he knew the judge was a fanatical Bible pusher, and that when he had realized that the Jewish man had no respect for the Bible, that's where he knew the case was his. Brennan and O'Neill were fit to be tied. They couldn't believe that I got off again.

Outside the courtroom they told whoever would listen that what had happened was a travesty of justice and that there was no justice for the cops; it was only for the crooks. That morning I thought I had gotten away with something, but as I look back, I was the loser because I had lost a little more respect for the law, something that I paid for later. At the time, though, I was convinced that with a good lawyer I could beat any charge laid against me.

It was around this time that Brennan approached me with a proposition that sounded pretty good. His district was in the heart of the city, approximately one square mile—one mile east and west, and one mile north and south. He told me that as long as I did not break and enter any stores or houses in his district, he would stop picking me up. He said he did not care how many places I robbed outside his district, just as long as I left his territory alone. I thought this to be a very good deal, so I accepted it and it paid off in more ways than one. I did not get picked up anymore for questioning, and I made just as many scores as before. In fact, Brennan ran into me one night when I and a friend were carrying a load of stolen goods, and he ignored us. The arrangement was to our mutual benefit.

Around this time, I was introduced to two new drugs: Benzedrine inhalers and pills, and Nembutals. I started by taking the Benzedrine pills. They were called "bennys" or "pep pills," and I noticed right away that I could stay up all night and take a couple more pills the next morning and not be tired at all. In fact, I could stay up three or four days at a time. They also made me talk a lot I just could not seem to stop talking. I remember telling my friends, before I met up with Benzedrine, not to talk too much. I told them that the penitentiaries were full of people who talked too much, and yet now I could not heed my own advice.

I also found out that I could get a better high

by taking the sniffer out of a Benzedrine inhaler, adding a little hot water to the cotton sponge inside, pounding it until I had dissolved the amphetamines into the water and then sucking up the solution with a syringe and shooting it into my mainline veins. I got a lot higher this way, but found it harder to sleep. Someone suggested that I get some "yellow-jackets" or Nembutals, which I did, and from then on I could sleep when I wanted to.

When I took bennys and Nembutals together they made me react as if I were drunk. But I could not leave the house, and I had a hard time just making it to the washroom. At this time my drug addiction became obvious to my friends and family, so I moved again and went to live with my brother Cy. After I moved in, I found out he was still shooting up, and it was not long before I decided to try a fix of heroin. I was scared of heroin and morphine because I had seen the way my brother suffered when he could not get a fix or when he had a bad trip. I had experienced highs on grass, hash, bennys, and Nembutals. but Cy had told me that if I wanted a better high than any other I had experienced, then I would have to try heroin. So without much serious thought to the consequences, I began shooting heroin. I got really high, it was an experience I shall never forget, and it soon became obvious that I was hooked.

Cy took the time to explain what a wonderful high I would get, but what he forgot to tell me was that heroin would also take me to the depths of hell and that I would get to know suffering such as I had never known before. I now believe that he got me to take those heroin trips with him because he couldn't bear to take them alone.

One of the side effects of heroin on me was the way it slowed me down. My thinking became slower and my actions sluggish. My timing was so far off that I had to adapt to a new personality. I was in a daze most of the time.

I had to make more money to feed my habit. I soon got arrested for some type of robbery and I got thrown into Bordeaux Jail, where I went through withdrawal pains. I can't describe the suffering I went through. I only know that I folded myself into the smallest position I could on the cell floor and shook and suffered and screamed and prayed that God would have mercy on me and take my life. Death would have been a wonderful relief from the hell I was going through.

That was something else I did not understand. I told everyone that I did not believe in God, in fact I claimed to be an atheist, yet whenever I found myself in deep trouble I called on God for help. I guess it was Mom's example. Anytime she could not cope with a situation, she asked God's help and claimed that he always helped her.

I had not experienced real suffering from drugs until this time, although I do remember getting very scared a few times. For example, one beautiful sunny July afternoon, I went over to see Cy at his small apartment, hoping that he had something that we could get high on. He was not in, but I got in by a window and found some old Benzedrine inhalers. The absorbent that held the amphetamines had been pounded up and used quite often, but I decided to mix them all together and see if I could get a fix. After I had injected myself, I started to get cold and my teeth started to chatter. I can remember only one other time that I got that cold, and that was when I was a kid and took the freight train out of Toronto, running away from reform school. Since this time the outside temperature was at least ninety-five degrees Fahrenheit, I was scared.

I thought I had shot some air into my veins. Cy had warned me often that this would likely kill me. When you suck up the liquid that you are going to shoot in a syringe, after you've attached the needle, there is usually an air bubble at the bottom of the syringe and before you stick it in your vein you are supposed to tap the bottom of the syringe with your finger to bring the air bubble to the top. I was afraid that I must have forgotten to tap the syringe, and that I was going to die. I rushed out and headed home.

I was freezing when I got there. I met my brother, Bob, told him what had happened, and asked him if he would get me some extra blankets. As I lay in my Mom's bed, I was sure that I was going to die. Bob and my sister, Theresa, covered me with every blanket they could find—I was still freezing. I guess I passed out. When I came to it was night and the bed was soaking wet with sweat.

I soon realized where I was, and as my eyes became accustomed to the darkness I saw the shape of a person on her knees at the foot of the bed, and I knew right away that it had to be my Mother. Mom's favourite saying was, "There is more wrought by prayer than this world dreams of," and she was practicing what she preached. Poor Mom, she was always there when I needed her. You might think that such experiences would have stopped me from shooting drugs, but no. I could not learn from my mistakes.

There were other things happening to me that I found strange. I lost track of days—days when I did not remember a thing. I went through terrible nightmares that seemed real. In retrospect, I believe that my life had become a nightmare. Cy had told me some hair-raising tales about the asylum, St. Jean de Dieux—one patient was beaten unconscious and thrown in the hole, and when they opened his door the next morning they found him dead with his nose eaten away by rats. I had heard many similar stories from friends of Cy, friends who had spent some time in St. Jean de Dieux, and I was terrified at the thought of ending up there for the rest of my life.

One sunny afternoon, Detective O'Neill found me sleeping on St. Catherine Street. What was odd was that he swore I was standing and leaning against the wall of a department store. He said I was sound asleep and snoring, with a crowd of people watching and two guys taking bets on how long it would be before I fell down. I had been stiff before, but this was ridiculous. O'Neill told me later that the crowd was really pissed off when he woke me up. I am sure they must have thought that a man in my position should not be disturbed. O'Neill and my friends ribbed me a lot after this, asking questions such as "What street are you going to sleep on tonight?"

It was around this time that a friend and I made a big score from a beautiful, large home on the side of the mountain. We crawled into a bed-room window and found a jewellery box full of beautiful expensive jewellery. As soon as I saw it I knew that we had struck pay dirt, so we made a quick exit.

We found a fence and realized about four thousand dollars for all of the jewellery, except one man's ring, which I fell in love with and kept. That ring was made up of two dice—one a four and the other a three—with seven diamonds. "Lucky seven," I thought. I imagined that it would bring me luck—and I believe that it did. The next day, when we looked in the newspapers to find out if the robbery had been reported, we found that we had been suckered again. The victims said that they had lost sixty-eight thousand dollars worth of jewellery, but all we got for it was four. We knew that many victims claimed to have lost more than they really did so that they could collect more insurance, but I was pretty sure that we got less than ten percent of the real value.

We shot up and celebrated for a week or so until we ran out of money and had to get back to work.

I soon got arrested for another robbery, and when the cops took my personal effects at the desk, they noticed the diamond ring. It was not long before they found out that it was part of the sixty-eight thousand dollar robbery, and so they questioned me all night. Finally I got an idea. I told them that if they let me out for forty-eight hours I would bring back all the jewellery. I told them that since I did not want to get anyone in trouble, I could not tell them where the jewellery was. The sergeant detective said he would talk to Captain O'Neill and let me know. He returned and took me to Captain O'Neill's office. O'Neill said that he did not trust me, but suggested that if the detectives who had arrested me wanted to take a chance on me, then he would leave the case up to them. They decided to take a chance, so I was released.

They released me on a Thursday evening and I was supposed to return Saturday night. I certainly had no intention of giving myself up and so on Saturday afternoon I left for Toronto with a couple of friends. We started looking for places to rob and decided on an A & P store. This was part of a popular chain of grocery stores at the time. We had spotted a small safe and we calculated that it wouldn't weigh more than three or four hundred pounds. We stole a car and returned late at night with the idea of stealing the safe, putting it into the car, taking it out to the country and busting it open.

We soon realized that we had not planned too well. For one thing, as soon as we smashed open the back window of the store, the alarm went off, which really surprised us because we had checked the store out and been sure that it was not bugged. Then when we got to the safe we found that it was bolted to the floor. We didn't have time to break it loose, so we decided to grab as much as we could carry and run. The others got in and out fast, but by the time I was ready to leave I could see the cops out front shining their flashlights in. I knew the gig was up. They spotted me and, because they had the front and back covered, there was nothing to do but give up. They took me to a police station and questioned me for a few hours, trying to find out who I was with. I told them nothing, so they charged me with breaking and entering and locked me up in the Don Jail.

One thing that stands out in my mind is that everyone in there seemed to be complaining and bitching about the food. I thought the food and the conditions were great because I was comparing the place with Mont St-Antoine École de Réforme and Bordeaux Jail—actually there was no comparison. At least at the Don we got out of our cells, could play cards on tables in the cell block and were only locked up at night, whereas in Bordeaux we were locked up twenty-four hours a day while awaiting trial. On a scale of one to ten, Mont St.-Antoine would be a one, Bordeaux a two, and the Don Jail about a six.

I was not at the Don very long before I appeared before a judge. I pleaded guilty and was remanded for a week. Then I was sentenced to Guelph Reformatory for one year. I was pleasantly surprised when I arrived at Guelph. It was a prison for first offenders and old prisoners, and the most severe sentence you could get there was two years less a day. All the jails I had seen were as different as night and day. Bordeaux was run on the same system as the Bastilles (prisons) in France: lots of beatings and punishments. Guelph, by contrast, was run in a humane and intelligent manner. When I arrived at the Don Jail I was scared because I knew I would have to go through withdrawal pains from the drugs I had been using. But it was not nearly as bad as I thought because they gave me some shots that kept me so drowsy I ended up sleeping most of the time. At Guelph the doctor weaned me off the drugs by giving me shots of Methadone.

I also ended up eating at the hospital because I told the doctor that I had a pin ulcer, and he believed me. Although the food was terrific in

Guelph, eating in the hospital was better because we got as much as we wanted. We did not have to stand in line and we were close to the drugs, which we were always trying to score. I became good at gambling and was very lucky. At that time tobacco was bought and sold at five decks for a buck, and lighters sold from one deck to five. I became so lucky at a game called "To Me To You" (it was Evens or Odds) that it seemed I could not lose. All the good gamblers ended up playing at the hospital.

I had an assistant at the time, and all he did was pick up the tobacco as I won it and shove it into a pillowcase. I had a job getting rid of the tobacco because I could only store so many pillowcases around the hospital. I soon possessed a fairly big bankroll, and when you have money in the can you get more respect and consideration. I also knew the right hands to place some of this money in, and so I could do no wrong; I seemed to have the run of the place.

I was also getting drugs into the place by using a couple of the screws. I got amphetamines, known on the street as "speed," in the form of an inhaler or as pills, without a prescription. I also got Seconals, Nembutals, and a few others without too much trouble, and so I had another method of making a buck. My bankroll grew. I was paying something like a dime for a benny and selling it for fifty cents. I was also selling other drugs at a good profit.

My big worry was how to get rid of the money I was making. I never could trust anyone. Whenever I had trusted a few people in the past I had always got screwed; but I had to trust someone so I decided to trust a screw. I began unloading the money on him. He was my contact. He could get me nearly anything I wanted. His name was Doogin and he had emigrated from Ireland. He was always laughing and joking; everyone liked him. He was loud and very talkative when I met him, but when he eventually got hooked on amphetamines we couldn't shut him up.

I smashed up a couple of bennys one day and put the powder into his coffee. We were shocked at the results. He seemed to explode, and wanted to climb the walls. I had never seen anyone react the way he did, and I was a little envious that I couldn't get a high like that. It was not long before he was hooked on a few others, such as Seconals and Nembutals, drugs that brought him back to earth.

The drugs affected his efficiency. His dress became sloppy, his speech slurred and he wasn't as careful as he had been before. One morning while he was bringing in some swag he was stopped and searched. They found some drugs on him and so he was charged with possession of drugs for the purpose of trafficking. I have always felt bad about Doogin. I had a guilty conscience for a long time. I felt that I was behind all his troubles. He pleaded guilty to the charges, and was sentenced to two years in the penitentiary and ordered deported when released.

Life at Guelph never was the same again. After he left, the other screws were afraid to bring in anything because of what had happened to Doogin, and so there was a great shortage of drugs in the prison. There was a lot of fighting between inmates and one could feel the tension in the air. Then one night all hell broke loose.

The inmates were lined up to go into the big dining area for supper. Apparently the kitchen was short of potatoes and refused to give out second helpings. This was enough to start a riot. I could not help thinking that if these dummies ever had to eat the slop at Mont St.-Antoine or Bordeaux Jail they would certainly appreciate what they had. (My mouth still waters when I think of the corn fritters they used to serve us; I have yet to find corn fritters that compare with them. Also, the barbecued spareribs and other foods that the chef prepared were superb.) I am sure that most of those characters never ate that well in their lives.

As a result of the riot, a lot of inmates were punished, and I was one of them. The screws searched me and found some drugs, so they gave me six strokes of the paddle and threw me into the hole. I had heard so much about the dreaded limbo room where they strapped you down and gave you the paddle, but after getting the *banan* so often at Mont St.-Antoine, I figured it couldn't be much worse. I was happy to find out that it was not.

I was surprised to find that the "hole" was on the third floor, underneath the hospital. They took me up in the elevator, let me off at the third floor and locked me in a nice spacious cell with bars. I immediately got in touch with Danny, the hospital cook, by yelling out my window, and he sent me down a couple of sandwiches on a horse (a rope or string with a hook on the end of it).

Their worst punishment was a lot easier than the punishments that I received at the reform school, when I was ten and eleven years of age, and here they even held a hearing and let you defend yourself. This was so different from what I had been used to. Other inmates could not understand why I thought that the punishment they gave me was fair.

I soon realized that most inmates are compulsive complainers. I was as much a complainer as any of them, only my level of acceptance was different because of where I'd been before. The difference between Bordeaux Jail and Guelph Jail was the same as the difference between staying at a fleabag hotel on Queen Street and staying at the Royal York. I've heard that it is not good to compare, but in my case I was very grateful for my new, higher standard of living. If the inmates here had received a taste of the reform school in Montreal or the Bordeaux Jail, they would have appreciated Guelph a lot more.

I spent about a week in the hole. After that I tried to stay out of trouble because I had been warned that if I gave them any more trouble they would deduct the "good time" from my one-year sentence. I had done ten months and eight days, and I was anxious to get out as soon as possible. I continued to gamble but I stopped pushing drugs; so when I asked the sergeant for a transfer to the farm, he gave his permission.

I spent the rest of my time out in the sun, and met one of the best screws in the joint. Hobson was not strict on the rules and he never put anyone on report. We had a lot of fun. We worked hard, but when we had finished our work we went up to the barn to play cards or just lie out in the sun. My time was nearly finished and so I was careful not to get into any trouble. Although I was still getting high on painkillers and bennys, as long as I did not act too strangely, Hobson looked the other way. All in all I felt that Guelph was a wonderful experience, and when the day came for my release I actually felt bad about leaving some of the good friends I had made there.

A few days before I was released I had to solve the problem of getting my money out. I thought I had come up with a couple of bright ideas. One of them was to send a letter addressed to myself care of general delivery in Toronto, and to get Hobson to register it for me and give me the receipt. So I sent a couple of hundred that way and the rest of my money I buried under some tomato plants with the idea of returning at night to get it back. I also was able to sneak about a hundred dollars out with me.

When I got to Toronto I went to the general delivery office, where the clerk gave me a hard time because I did not have much identification. When he finally handed over my letter, I found that it contained only the two sheets of paper I had wrapped the money in. I thought of a maxim that I heard in the carnival: "Never give a sucker an even break." Man, was I ever a sucker. I found out later that I had not been gone an hour before they had found my money under the tomato plants.

CHAPTER SIX

UNWANTED

When I got out, what I needed most of all was a woman and I met one that first night. Her name was Marjorie, and by a crazy coincidence she was from Montreal and knew one of my sisters, Joan. We hit it off right away and what I had been dreaming about for over three hundred days and nights finally came to pass. I think we stayed in bed for three days and nights.

I had always thought of myself as a great lover (until I found out the true meaning of love) and Jeannine, the beautiful French woman I met when I was delivering groceries, impressed on me how important it was to always be tender with a woman, and also how important foreplay was. I was never gifted with much patience, but when it came to making love to a woman it was important to me that I had to be the best. Oh, how I loved to hear a woman say that I was the best she ever had! Oh, how proud I was when my back was so badly scratched that I had the scars for weeks.

I believe that I was gripped by a new obsession—I had to own women. I bragged that I could satisfy any woman sexually. I did not realize how sick I really was, so I went along my merry way only to find out later that this was just another monkey on my back.

I returned to Montreal, and was excited at the thought of seeing good old Mom and the rest of the family. But trouble seemed to follow me wherever I went. It was Sunday morning when I arrived and Mom and the old man were at church. I had been away for over a year and the family was glad to see me. In jail I had dreamed of coming home, finding a job, going straight and making Mom proud of me. At seventeen years of age, I still had lots of hope for my future.

I was sitting at home, waiting for my family to return from church, when suddenly the front door opened and in walked my old man. I stuck out my hand, thinking and hoping that we would be friends, but as soon as he saw me he started screaming at me and calling me rotten names. I went into a rage. I punched him in the face and continued punching him until the family dragged me off him. Mom came home in the middle of it and made me leave. She also found me a room that day. I remember thinking that even with the very best of intentions, I could not stay out of trouble. It was depressing.

My sister Kay at this time had met a wonderful guy called Ken. Ken had just graduated from McGill University as an engineer. He had heard that I was coming home from Toronto, and had suggested to Kay, whom he planned to marry, that because they were going to New York for the weekend, it would be a good idea to invite Mom and me to accompany them. I thought it was a great idea. Many times I had dreamed of travelling—to New York, Chicago, Boston ….

I was excited and did not sleep much until the day we left. We had an uncle, Patrick Maloney, who owned a big house on Staten Island, where we stayed. He also owned a nice big bar. We arrived on Friday evening, danced, drank and celebrated in his bar, and later at his home, until the early hours of the morning.

Saturday, before noon, we caught the Staten Island Ferry and found ourselves in New York City. We had lunch and then went to Radio City Music Hall, where we were all impressed with the Rockettes, and the beautiful theatre. Ken suggested that we all have dinner in a beautiful restaurant on Broadway. The only drawback was that men had to wear a shirt and tie and I was wearing a sweater. Mom fixed this up by buying me a shirt and tie.

We entered the restaurant. It was quite a classy joint. The headwaiter directed us to a lovely table and a waiter came over, took our orders and returned shortly with bowls. My Mom and I, who were quite hungry from all the walking we had done, dug right in. I remember remarking to my Mom what lousy soup it was, that it tasted just like water. She told me to squeeze some more lemon into it.

Suddenly I got a kick from under the table. My immediate reaction was to kick back even harder—we always did that at home. Kay let out a holler. As she jumped to her feet to get at me she accidentally knocked over the table. I grabbed a knife to defend myself, but thank God the waiters subdued us before things got worse. We were all thrown out, but I'll never forget the stunned look on poor Ken's face. The trip back to Montreal was very quiet, and I never saw Ken again. I don't think Kay did either. On the way back we also found out why Kay was so upset. She said she was never so embarrassed in her life as when we began eating the contents of the fingerbowls.

What I regret most is that this was the only holiday that Mom and I ever went on together, and I'm sure that it was the only holiday that Mom ever had.

Upon returning to Montreal, it wasn't too long before I was arrested for the old charges, which I had run away from. The police held me for a while and then decided to let me go. I guess they had made a few mistakes and they did not want them brought out in the courtroom. It was not long before I was back with my old friends and operating as before. I was back on drugs, but with a difference—I wouldn't touch heroin, morphine, or hard drugs. I still shot up a little, but only with amphetamines, and occasionally I snorted cocaine. I also kept a good supply of Nembutals handy because I used these to make a score.

I got a job in a nightclub called the Night Cap. The owner was a guy called "Johnny the Wop," and although he couldn't read or write he was a good businessman. Just about anything went in this place. I started as a busboy and soon became a part-time waiter. The Night Cap was always full of people. In fact, there was usually a line-up at the front door. These were the good times, 1943, and there was lots of money around. Plenty of service-

men and civilians were living it up. I had a girlfriend whom I went out with after work, and we
went to other clubs to drink and dance. This cost
money, of course, so I had to find a way to make
more money.

I think it was the second night I worked as a
waiter that one of my customers fell asleep on me.
When this happened we were supposed to wake
the customer and lead him or her outside. Well, I
had noticed when I served him a drink which
pocket he kept his money in, and it wasn't too hard
to clean out the pocket as I helped him outside.

I was doing very well with tips, but I figured
that if more customers passed out, then it would
only be natural that I could roll more of them and
make more money. So I started spiking their drinks
with Nembutals—making a Mickey—and after
they'd downed that and passed out, they were
much easier to handle. Things were going great
until one morning, after work, Johnny the Wop
told me to not bother coming back that night, or
any other night. I tried to find out why he was letting me go, but he only said, "I don't like your
work." I found out from the other waiters that too
many people had been passing out in my section
of the club, and that Johnny was getting too many
people complaining of being robbed. I was really

sorry about leaving the Night Cap and wished I had played my cards differently.

I was soon back to my other bad habits and would do anything for a buck because I always needed money for a fix or a party. It wasn't long before I was back in jail. One thing about jail is that if you had a little money you could always get drugs and that made your time a lot easier. In Bordeaux Jail you could get anything if you had the money. With enough cash you could choose your own cell, buy special food and even get booze.

Some inmates had more authority than the guards, and many times when I wanted something picked up on the outside I arranged it with an inmate; the next day I would receive what I had ordered. Inmates could also get drugs at the hospital, but they were more expensive than having drugs smuggled in.

It was obvious to everyone that many of the inmates were nearly always high, but it seemed that the screws and the senior authorities just ignored what was going on. I have always believed that the prison administration encouraged drugs to a certain extent because drugged inmates became passive and were a lot less trouble.

Other inmates made home brew. The screws

frowned on this because when prisoners got drunk they generally fought or caused other trouble, so the staff tried to keep a tight rein on the booze.

In each wing of the prison, the screws had a corporal in charge. The corporal picked one of the toughest inmates to be captain of the wing, and put him in the number one cell, giving him all kinds of favours and special treatment for keeping the other inmates in line. This was a job that many of the toughest prisoners were willing to fight for, and I saw some of the most vicious fights of my life during such contests. They were like a fight to the death, with the winner in some cases unable to accept his reward because he was so badly injured in the fight.

One particular captain, Johnny Young, was the toughest inmate in my wing and had a really bad reputation. He had been a well-known bouncer in some of the roughest dives on the Main Street in downtown Montreal. When he was given the job of wing captain, no one challenged him, but after a few months a big Frenchman arrived at the jail— a former lumberjack, who had put two policemen in hospital. He must have weighed at least two hundred and fifty pounds. When he heard that the job of captain of the wing went to the toughest con he started getting ideas and a lot of the inmates kept encouraging him to take his rightful place in cell number one. He did not need much convincing because he was sure that he could beat Johnny Young. He weighed about sixty pounds more than Johnny and was also a lot bigger in size, and Johnny did not look tough.

One Saturday morning when our time came to go down for a shower, the prisoners talked of nothing else but the big fight that was going to take place; the screws were making bets with each other on who was going to win. The inmates were also betting all they had on the outcome. Each man had his own rooting section, as well as supporters who tried to find weaknesses in the opponent, and then passed these on to their gladiator to improve his chances of victory.

Most of the Johnny Young supporters knew what Johnny could do in a fight. He had been fighting on the waterfront and in some of the toughest dives in Montreal for years, but Taureau Dubé was an unknown quantity. A few of the inmates from his part of the country sang his praises, but from what I could see most of his reputation came from self-praise, which was not worth too much in a fight.

We were standing in line in the change room, waiting for our clean clothes before we entered the

shower and everything was nice and quiet. Then
Johnny came in and walked past us to the head of
the line to get his clothes first. This was one of the
privileges that went with the territory.

Taureau Dubé yelled from his place in line for
Johnny to get to the back of the line or he would
break his fucking neck. Johnny put the clothes he
had been given back on the counter and walked
back down the line. The line disintegrated and we
all took positions at the other end of the room
where we could watch the fight. It was one of the
dirtiest fights that I ever want to see. It actually
made me and a few others sick.

Johnny was the type of guy who really got his
jollies from exercising. Every time you looked into
his cell he was doing push-ups or chin-ups or
handstands. He loved having a strong body, could
not stand having an ounce of fat on him, so he continually worked out, whereas Taureau, or "Bull"
Dubé, as he was called, might have once been as
strong as a bull when he was working in the bush,
but drinking and lying around for a year had taken
a lot of his strength.

When Johnny got to where Taureau was standing, the Bull looked more like a lamb. I guess the
full impact of his predicament suddenly dawned
on him. He jumped into a fighting stance and

Johnny advanced on him. Johnny's open hand shot out and his two middle fingers were spread just enough to enter the Bull's eyes. The next thing I saw was one of the Bull's eyes out of its socket, lying on his cheek. I felt really sick at the sight. There were a few guards in the room, but they made no move to stop the fight.

To this day, I am sure that Bull Dubé did not know that his eye was out of the socket—he kept on trying to make a fight of it. And I am sure that he soon realized that he was no match for Johnny. He was taking a terrible beating, and most of the inmates were telling Johnny to beat him more. The last thing I saw before I got sick and had to leave the room was Johnny kicking and stomping on the Bull's face, and the big eyeball bouncing all around.

I later heard the ambulance as they carted poor Bull away. I often wonder whether he died as a result of that fight. I know that I suffered as a result of seeing it, because I have seen that eyeball in my drug-crazed mind, in many of my nightmares, and when I have had attacks of the DTs. I guess the memory of that fight will never leave me.

What I found strange was that the supporters of Dubé, guards and inmates, could switch their support so fast when they realized that their gladiator was losing. It was as though Taureau Dubé had let them down by not winning, so now they could switch their allegiance to Johnny and yell for him to kill the bastard.

I cannot tell you whether Dubé lived or died as a result of that fight because I never saw him again. But Johnny became so paranoid and vicious after that fight that he turned into a wild animal. He ended up in the hole at St. Vincent de Paul Penitentiary after attacking a guard, and was transferred to Kingston Penitentiary, where I heard he died in solitary confinement.

At Bordeaux there were different kinds of punishments. If the offence was not too serious they threw you into a "deadlock," that is, locked you in your cell twenty-four hours a day with no books or cigarettes or anything else. The cell was completely closed in, there was a small window that looked out into the yard and a large steel door with a tiny peephole that you could barely get your small finger through. I came to appreciate that little hole when I was deadlocked, and I would stand by it all day looking out, hoping that someone would pass by and give me a cigarette.

Then there was the other punishment: they threw you into the hole. There was a wooden contraption, about six inches off the floor, where you were supposed to sleep, eat, sit, and anything else you wanted to do on it. You were given bread and water once a day, and a baloney sandwich every three days. There was no natural way to tell if it was day or night because there was no light. When they brought the bread and water you figured it was morning, and you counted the days by the number of times they fed you.

This was really terrifying for prisoners who were afraid of rats or mice. I had not been afraid of rats when I was younger and slept under the verandas, but I became terrified of them in jail. We had small toilet bowls in our cells, and the rats came in through there. I had heard a lot of stories about some of the inmates who had been bitten, and some who had died as a result of being bitten. I had seen some of the scars left on inmates from rat bites, and you can be sure that my first trip to the hole was a terrifying experience.

I was given seven days for fighting and I sat against the wall the whole seven days. All I could hear was the moaning, groaning, and screaming of the inmates who were suffering from the beatings they had received from the screws. That was one method of punishment that was performed by the most sadistic and inhumane bunch of bastards that

I have ever seen.

These were the enforcers—the biggest, ugliest, cruellest screws in the prison. To qualify as an enforcer you had to weigh at least two hundred and fifty pounds, be as cruel and sadistic as possible and love the sight of blood. They all worked the night shift, and the inmates feared these maniacs most of all. I remember standing by my cell door all night, looking out the peep hole and listening for any sound that might warn me of their presence. I have often wondered how many other inmates stood by their cell doors looking and listening, and hoping that they would not be the next victim.

I watched these sadistic bastards sneak up to a cell door between one and four in the morning. One put the key in the lock and very quietly unlocked the door, then slid it open as fast as possible so the others could rush in and take the victim by surprise. There was always one screw for each leg, one for each arm and two to apply the beating as they dragged the prisoner along the marble floor and down the steel steps to the hole. They used a blackjack and a billy club, and the agonized screams of the victim filled me with such fear that I was unable to sleep the rest of the night.

I know that some of the inmates, as a result of

this type of torture, ended up in the bug wing, which was a part of the prison for the criminally insane. This wing was supposed to hold two hundred prisoners but was always overcrowded. God only knows how many prisoners died as a result of these beatings, but it was a common sight to see a dead body on a stretcher in the basement, waiting to be picked up by the truck from the morgue.

There were quite a few hangings and suicides and a lot of gory deaths at Bordeaux Jail. One botched-up hanging that got a lot of publicity was of a very large woman who was sentenced to hang. She weighed over three hundred pounds. The hangman put the noose around her neck and stood her on the trapdoor. When he sprung the trap and she dropped, her head couldn't hold the weight of her body and so her head and body went in different directions. I witnessed all this from my cell window.

Some inmates went up to the third tier and jumped off onto the marble floor below. The remains would be shovelled up and the floor hosed down to get rid of the blood. One thing that I have always found hard to believe is that all the deaths were caused by accidents, suicides, natural causes, or legal executions. Some of the bodies that lay in the basement were well-wrapped and had straps around them, while others lay uncovered. I was always curious to know what the body under the covers looked like, but if you were smart you did not ask too many questions. You remained much healthier when you minded your own business.

The hole was one of my worst fears because I was claustrophobic. I dreaded the thought of being locked in a cell or a small place—even the sight of a straitjacket upset me. I had seen inmates who lost their tempers and flew into a rage or panic, attacked guards or attempted to, and ended up in a straitjacket in the hole. One day my worst fear was realized.

I was standing at my cell window talking to a guy in English when this creep who lived further along the tier began calling me names and telling me to speak French. We started arguing and cursing back and forth. I should have kept my big mouth shut because suddenly there was a loud knock on my cell door. I ran to the door and peered out of the little peephole, to find that the guy was on the other side. He spat through the hole and caught me smack in the face. I lost it and began kicking the door and making a commotion. To make it worse, I could hear him laughing at me.

I can't remember ever losing my head as completely as I did that day. I don't know how he got out of his cell, but a screw arrived on the scene and escorted him away, and the two of them shared a joke as he did so. My rage increased.

A while later, supper was brought to our cells. This involved one screw opening the doors, followed by three inmates holding two trays each. Another screw followed up behind. This meant that while the supper trays were being delivered to our cells, there were at least five cell doors open between the two screws. As my cell door was being unlocked, I could see my antagonist standing in the door of his cell, still laughing. Something snapped, and before I knew it I was in his cell battering him to the floor. I had so much hate and frustration in me that I could not think straight or even care about the consequences of my actions. I tried to kill him.

By the time the guards arrived, there was plenty of blood in the cell, and none of it was mine. The prison staff said that I had acted like a wild man, so they decided to treat me as one. I was put into a straitjacket and thrown into the hole. The hole was six feet by eight feet, with a cement floor and plaster walls. It had a board raised off the floor for sleeping on, and a pail in the corner. The marble toilet had been smashed to bits long ago. The worst thing of all was that the hole was infested with rats, mice and cockroaches. There had been a time when these things didn't bother me, but ever since hearing that some inmates had lost ears and the odd nose to rats, I was not simply scared—I was petrified.

I was thrown into the cell and landed on my face. I lay there with my arms tied behind my back, and my legs tied together. The jacket was so tight that I found it hard to breathe. The cell was pitch black, and with every sound I grew more frightened. After repeated efforts to roll onto my back I became exhausted. For the longest time I had been yelling so as to scare away the rats and mice, but eventually my voice went hoarse and all I could do was growl. It was a growl to put most animals to shame.

I had heard that animals can detect fear in a person, so I was trying to put more fear into them than they were putting into me. I was alarmed that I could sound like a ferocious beast, but I should not have been all that surprised, considering the jungle that I grew up in.

I thought that night would never end. I did manage to get onto my back, but my efforts to sit up or stand up were unsuccessful. Suddenly, I heard the sound of doors opening and knew that slop time had arrived. My door opened and I was given a mug of tea and a bun. Luckily the bun landed near my head, but the hard part was getting it into my mouth. I struggled to get into the best position next to the bun only to find that because it was round and hard, I couldn't get it between my teeth. After several failed attempts, I rolled onto my back exhausted, and flattened the roll with the back of my head. I was able to eat it after that.

That first experience of life in a straightjacket has remained with me and has been the source of many subsequent nightmares. I was told later that the screws would have released me from the jacket sooner, but they had thought from the way I was growling that doing so would not have made any difference because they thought I was crazy.

Seven days later my sentence was finished, so I had many better things to think of, and the day finally arrived when I was released from jail. The first thing I did was visit my brother Cyril and get a fix. Then I met some of the guys and started drinking. Most of the addicts I knew did not mix drugs and booze, but I just could not seem to get enough of anything.

I don't remember too much about that day, but I will never forget the next day: I awoke to the sound of slamming steel doors. I could not believe that I was back in jail! I lay there with my eyes closed and tried to recall what happened the night before but I could not remember anything. I had been in a complete blackout, and was worried sick about what I had done. I opened my eyes and soon realized that I was in a cellblock in the Detective Section. This meant that I must have committed a criminal offence; they kept the drunks in the bullpen. I was charged with possession of stolen goods.

The cop at the desk would not tell me anything, so I just had to wait until the dicks that had brought me in came to see me. On mornings like this, and I had a few of them, I would really go through hell worrying about whether I had carried a gun the night before, and if I might have used it.

I found out that they had picked me up for breaking and entering, and that they had found me with some stolen property. Actually it was a relief to find out what I had been charged with. Apparently I had also signed a confession, something I would never have done had I been in my right mind. I was taken to court right away and had to plead guilty, but I was lucky: the judge only sentenced me to seven months. And so I was back in Bordeaux Jail one day after getting out.

Oh, how discouraged and depressed I felt being driven back to Bordeaux in the paddy wagon after only one day of freedom from a six-month sentence. Now I was returning for seven more months. My depression remained with me until the day I was released. During that time I did a lot of thinking, and became convinced that it was my drinking and drug use that had brought me all this trouble. I determined to keep away from drugs and to cut down on my drinking. At least I would try.

As the days went by in jail, I became more and more confident that I could do it. After my release I went looking for a job, and it was not too long before I found one. Someone told me that I should fill out an application at the railroad for the dining car department. Apparently they were looking for waiters, cooks, and kitchen help. The idea of travelling to different cities really appealed to me.

Well, they hired me, and that was the first decent job I ever had. My job was pantry man, and my duties were to wash dishes and prepare the side dishes that the waiters needed during the meal. Oh, how I loved this job! As I look back I am sure that I spent some of the happiest days of my life on the railroad. My run was from Montreal to Capreol, Ontario. We would leave Montreal around four P.M., arrive in Ottawa about seven P.M., spend about four hours there, then leave for Capreol, arriving there about eight-thirty A.M. There we switched dining cars. Our diner and the Winnipeg diner would lay over for twenty-four hours while two other diners took our place going east and west. We would be sidetracked and be free to do whatever we wanted until the next morning.

Capreol was a small railroad town and nearly everyone who lived there worked for the railroad. There was not much of a business section. The Capreol Hotel and the Chinese restaurant beside it were the main attractions. The first thing I noticed when I went into the Chinese restaurant was a cute little waitress. She was about sixteen, and I think I fell in "love" with her at first sight. Her name was Judy, and we seemed to like each other from the start. She told me she was working part-time, filling in for another girl who was sick, and that she finished work at four o'clock. I asked her if I could see her after work and she said yes. She had been going out with the pantry man whom I had replaced, and I just took over where he left off.

Judy was French, and what she lacked in experience she made up for in passion. Her brother had built a shack in the back of their home and Judy and I spent every minute we could in that shack. We had some wonderful times.

After six months, the novelty wore off and I returned to my old habits. I started drinking again, missed my train a couple of times, and so they dropped me from that run and put me on the call-board. The guys listed on their board were fill-ins, and called the job "running wild." I had been running wild ever since I could remember, so this was nothing new to me. They would call and ask if I was available for a run to Toronto, Winnipeg, New York or wherever, and I would grab the train when it was pulling out and be on my way. This prolonged my job for a few months because I did not have a tight schedule, but I was still popping pills and drinking and I knew that it was only a matter of time before drugs and alcohol caught up with me.

The railroad called me at different times for a trip, but I was either out or hung-over and couldn't go, so they dropped me from the callboard and told me to come in and pick up my cheques and unemployment insurance book, which meant I was fired. I had been really happy on the railroad, but like most fools, I did not realize how much I was losing until I had lost it. You could say that was the story of my life: every time I found some success, I would sabotage it with alcohol or drugs.

Since I had no job I went back to what I knew best—stealing. It became the same old merry-go-round. I was beginning to hate the life that I was living because there was too much pain. Who wants to suffer? It seemed as if I were digging myself a black hole, and I got more and more scared that I would not be able to climb out.

My Mother suggested that a good psychiatrist might be able to help me. The only thing wrong with that advice was that I did not know the difference between a good psychiatrist and a bad one. My Mother got in touch with a social worker, who got an appointment for me with a Dr. Henderson. All I remember about the doctor is that he gave me a prescription for some pills. I can't even recall what kind of pills they were, but they did not help me in any way. I still could not cope with my problems; in fact, I did not know what my problems were.

It is hard to find a solution to a problem when you don't know the cause. The psychiatrist asked me if I had ever felt unwanted as a child. I told him that I could not forget the terror and fear I had of my father, especially when he was drinking. I explained that I usually slept under the bed, and that if I heard my dad coming towards the bedroom I jumped out the window and took off. I also told him how my father seemed to enjoy letting me know how much he hated me. One time he sent me to his brother's farm, which was four hundred miles away. I was there for about a month, and when I returned home the family had moved, without leaving a forwarding address. Luckily, my sister's girlfriends knew where they had moved to and gave me their address. That feeling of being abandoned remained with me for many years.

How I hated the way I lived! I was caught up in a tornado and could not set my own course; I had to drift along on whatever path it would take me. I was determined, though, to keep trying to get out of its grip. I was again released from jail, and was more determined than ever to stay out.

I began looking for a new job. I went to a restaurant called the Victory Coffee Shop. They had placed an ad for a short-order cook, and I knew that type of work so I applied for it. Although I was informed that the job had already been given to someone else, I decided to stop for coffee, and sat at the counter where two pretty girls were sitting.

I hit the jackpot. I forget how the conversation started, but they told me that they were from out west and that they were working for a guy called Billy Jacks selling magazine subscriptions. They were making lots of money.

Dale and Doris liked their jobs, they said, because they both loved to travel, and with this job they were free to do what they wanted. I envied them. I asked how many other people were working for Billy. They said one other girl and one guy, adding that if I spoke to Billy he would probably give me a job. One of his girls had become lonesome and had gone back home the week before. I found my heart beating faster; I was very excited about this job.

I met Billy and got the job. He would pay me forty cents on the dollar if I sold a hundred dollars worth of magazine subscriptions a day. I could make forty dollars a day and that was damn good money in those days. The cook's job I had applied for paid forty dollars a week, so I was very glad to get this job. Billy told me that I would be working with Ralph, the other guy working for him, and he took me over to the Laurier Hotel where the crew reported each night after work. We sat down and ordered a beer, and before long Ralph and Joan, the other girl who worked for Billy, came in.

Ralph handed over his order book, which he called a receipt pad, and sixty dollars. Billy gave him back thirty. Joan had made a hundred and was given forty dollars. I was impressed. Ralph told me that he was getting fifty percent because he helped Billy in other ways and that if I did well I could also make fifty percent. I was excited and couldn't wait to get started.

The next morning I was at the restaurant. Ralph and Billy were there, and I was told to work with Ralph until I got familiar with the sales pitch. When the girls came in they seemed to be hung over so I left with Ralph. He told me that he and Billy had made up a sales pitch about the Merchant Navy—they were getting a lot of publicity because they did not get any gratuities or rehabilitation like the Army, Navy, and Air Force. Everyone was saying that they should be entitled to a grant from the government for serving in the war zone. The other services were getting a grant for a college education or to make a down payment on a home, or a cash settlement. The girls were also provided with a sales pitch, telling people how they were to be entered into a nurse's training program if they could get two hundred names.

The year was 1947, and there was a lot of money around. I found out that I was a born salesman. I would ring the doorbell and say, "Good afternoon, Mr. Smith, my name is Earl Maloney and I am in the Merchant Navy. I have a chance to get a training in diesel engineering if I can get two hundred names by the end of the month." Mr. Smith usually asked if it was a petition, and I replied, "Yes, but we have also been given a little revue, and we are asking the people who give us their names if they would be so good as to also accept our little revue for the two years of training, at only six cents a week. Now, Mr. Smith, I am sure you would not want me bothering you for six cents a week, so if you could take it for the two years at five dollars, or one year at three dollars, I would be forever grateful." The more people I called on, the easier it got, and soon I was so proficient that I got as many as ten homes in a row.

I had one gimmick that almost always worked, and that was namedropping. Whether I had sold to the neighbour next door or not, I always said that I had. It would go like this: "Mrs. Harris, I have just been to see all your neighbours, Mr. Doyle, Mrs. Collins, Mrs. Best, and they have all given me their support; I know I can count on your support too, can't I, Mrs. Harris?" People always want to do what their neighbours have done. Some of them said to me: "Well, I guess if they have all signed up, I will too."

I was always a good liar, but I must have been extra convincing at this because even when they started with a firm "No," I usually ended up with the sale. Soon I was getting fifty percent of the money I brought in.

At one point, I found out what Billy Jacks was making on us. The magazine that Billy was pushing was called "The Empire Digest," and the publisher apparently wanted so many units of circulation that it was willing to pay ninety percent commission. Billy only had to pay ten cents on the dollar. He was making fifty percent of every dollar the girls brought in, and forty percent on Ralph and me. When I figured out what Billy was making from our sales of the magazines, at least a hundred and fifty to two hundred dollars a day, I was really envious. And it was more or less legal.

About this time I started dating Dale, and we really hit it off. I knew she had a lot of influence over Doris so I began telling Dale that she should be getting at least fifty percent, and that Billy was getting more from each dollar she made than she was. My idea was to get both of the girls to believe Billy was cheating them, and, as I said before, I can be quite convincing.

The Christmas season was approaching, and Billy was talking more and more about flying home for Christmas. I also was making plans. Billy told us that while he was away he was putting Ralph in charge of the crew, and that he would return after New Year's. No sooner did Billy fly away than I began packing my bags. Dale and Doris were promised at least fifty percent if they would come and work for me, and they agreed; they were tired of being cheated.

My next move was to buy a couple of bottles of whiskey and go and call on Ralph with Dale and Doris. He was staying at the Laurier Hotel and we met him in the bar and suggested that we all go up to his room for a party. He was very agreeable, and the next phase of my plan was soon carried out. Ralph had all Billy's order books, and I wanted them before the girls and I left town. I left Ralph a couple of receipt pads and took the rest. We went to the bus depot and took a bus to Ottawa.

The three of us then began a continuous party that took us into many states and to towns and cities all across the country. We checked into the Ritz Hotel in Ottawa, and danced and drank the night away. Everything went according to Hoyle, and we all seemed to sell a lot better. We could also sleep until noon with no one to bother us. I remember thinking of the old saying, "I'm living the life of Riley."

At this particular time I believed that there was nothing better in life than wine, women and song; I had all three of them and was determined to enjoy every minute of it. What I did not realize was that I was an addictive person, and that I could not get enough of anything. The more sex I got, the more I wanted. The more booze I got, the more

I wanted. I was trying to squeeze every ounce of pleasure out of every moment, because all my life, whenever I got to really enjoy something, I always lost it. Rather than figure out why, I was bent on enjoying it while it lasted.

Dale was a hot young Ukrainian girl from Saskatchewan, and she could not get enough sex either, so I thought we were a good match. I could not believe that something as good as sex should be rationed or not used to the fullest. I thought that I was fortunate to be oversexed. The girls did not mind, and I can remember bragging that I had hidden qualities.

I think that, because of the miserable time I had spent in jails and reform schools, I kept trying to make up for lost time and catch up, but I have also come to realize that I had a very great hunger and was searching for **love**. Most of my life, it had seemed that I did not belong anywhere and I felt like the loneliest guy in the world. Now I felt that I had found a place, but I also felt that it was too good to be true, and I was afraid that I would wake up and find that it was just a dream.

At this time I was not taking any hard drugs, but I was still hooked on bennys, and was taking Nembutals occasionally, when I couldn't sleep. My drinking was still causing me problems. It seemed that every time I drank there was trouble. There would be fights and property damage. The more I drank, the more insane my actions became. Dale and Doris would tell me the next day of things that I had done the night before, and I could hardly believe them. I was surprised that they stayed with me.

My sex drive seemed to increase with my consumption of alcohol. I was becoming concerned with my obsession for sex, and thought that it might be a disease of the mind. I had been warned as a child that a person who played with himself would end up in a mental hospital, but I could not control myself. It really scared me at times because I knew that I was capable of raping a woman, and thought that some day I might.

I was getting lots of sex with Dale, and I was also getting my share at work. I had heard a lot of stories about the travelling salesman. Now I was living the part and I was very naive. One of my early experiences came when I knocked on a door and was invited in for coffee. The young woman was in her housecoat, and as we talked I learned that her husband was some sort of inspector for the government and was sent out of town a lot. As soon as we sat down and she poured me a cup of coffee she said, "When you knocked at the door I was just about to have a bath. Would you mind if I had it while you are having your coffee?" I said, "Of course I don't mind," and she headed for the bathroom. She went in, turned on the water, took off her housecoat, came out and walked across the hall to the bedroom. All she had on were her panties and bra. I got so excited I could hardly talk. She crossed the hall a second time, going back to the bathroom, and I could feel that my pants were wet; I knew what had happened.

She got into the tub and continued talking as though she was still sitting at the kitchen table. She had left the bathroom door open, and must have known what she was doing to me. I finally got up the nerve to ask if I could wash her back, and she said that I could. By this time I was panting, and by the time I got on my knees beside the bathtub I was too weak to wash her back. I was trembling and she could see that I was hurting. She must have understood because she got out of the tub, dried off and we walked into the bedroom, arm in arm. She was the type of woman that any man would remember. She should have married a man who came home every night.

On my rounds, whenever a woman answered the door, I thought of sex, and I tried every conceivable way to get her into bed. My mind was more on screwing them than it was on selling to them. I often thought that I was very fortunate in getting a woman when I needed one; I can imagine how it would feel to have this obsession and not be able to have a woman. I really feel bad for the poor guys who go to jail for indecent assault and rape and never really get to know why they committed the crime.

I have come to believe that seventy percent of prison inmates would not be in jail if they could have been treated for their alcohol, drug, sex, or similar problems before committing their crimes. People say that an ounce of prevention is worth a pound of cure, yet they will not provide the facilities or personnel to keep these people out of jail. Without prevention, prisoners' lives become a disaster, with little hope for recovery.

I soon realized that there were many frustrated women who could not talk about their problems with their families or close friends so they unloaded their troubles on me. I could not understand why they were telling me all these things, but I found out later that it does people a lot of good to talk to someone about a problem. When they get it off their chests they always feel better. So, when I look back, I hope that I helped someone along the way.

Two other things that happened in Ottawa that I will always remember. The Australian ambassador gave me fifty dollars as a donation to help me through training, and I called on thirteen doctors in the Medical Arts Building, sold twelve of them, and got a prescription. This convinced me that I was in the right business.

We soon left Ottawa and landed in Toronto, where we continued to have parties every night. We checked into the old Ford Hotel and, as I remember it, that was one of the few places that I felt respectable, after comparing myself with some of the other clients who were hookers, boosters, swindlers, and con artists. I felt right at home. We stayed in Toronto a long time because it was always one of my favourite cities—this trip was no exception. I was sleeping with Dale every night. We were what you would call "shacked up," but I was never satisfied with just one girl. When Dale was not around I was looking for someone else.

Our next stop was Hamilton where I met a girl named Linda, whom I fell madly in love with and saw every day. She worked in a five-and-dime store—I think it was Woolworth's—and I saw her at lunch-time and nearly every night. She was an only child, and also a virgin, and I felt that I had to have her. She was a beautiful and innocent little girl whom I took advantage of. I was becoming a professional liar and con artist. I guess I had always been a liar, but now as I lied more and more I began to feel guilty. The night we left Hamilton I was supposed to meet Linda, but I did not meet her or even phone her.

I also had sex with Doris for the first time in Hamilton. It was the second Sunday we were there and Dale wanted to see a movie. Doris wanted to wash some clothes and I, as usual, wanted to get laid. As soon as Dale left the hotel I started scheming on how to get Doris into bed. I bought some magazines and weekend newspapers—the *Toronto Star*, *Hamilton Spectator* and a few others—and brought them up to Doris' room and asked her if she would like to look at them with me. She said all right, but probably wished she hadn't because I sat on the bed with her; and there was no way I could control myself for very long in that situation. I made some advances, and she tried to be loyal to her best friend Dale, but I was very persistent and did not let her go until I got what I wanted.

Believe me when I say I felt terrible. I was very sorry for what happened and had a guilty conscience, but my overpowering need for sex, my mental obsession and my feelings dictated my actions and I didn't know how to control them. I did not realize at the time the damage that these actions were causing. I began to hate myself. I would often try to justify my actions and rationalize them, but I could not escape my obsessive thoughts, feelings, and actions. I had a very guilty conscience.

We left Hamilton and stopped at Brantford, London, and Sarnia. We were making lots of money, having lots of fun. One day I overheard Doris talking to Dale, and I have always wondered whether Doris wanted me to overhear what she said. I'll never really know, but Doris was asking Dale why she went out with me, and what she could possibly see in me. While Doris was talking, I got the impression that she must really hate me, so I started again trying to find a way to get Doris away from Dale overnight. I just had to have her, and I really believed that if I could get her to bed for the night she would change her opinion of me. Well, my plans worked perfectly.

Sarnia is a border town, and across the Blue Water Bridge is Port Huron, Michigan. I planned on getting Doris over there for a few drinks and keeping her for the night. I told Dale that we needed extra money, so we were going to work that evening. I sent her to one end of town and then got Doris to have a couple of drinks with me and accompany me to Port Huron. We checked into a nice club. Doris told the management that I was a good singer, so they asked me to come up and sing a song. I ended up singing three or four, and after that it was easy to get Doris up to the hotel room. I made love to Doris at least half a dozen times that night and her opinion of me sure changed. She moved in with me when we got back to Sarnia, and poor Dale had to live alone.

This may sound egotistical but if there was one thing that I could do right it was to make love to a woman. I really adored them, appreciated them, and would jump off the Brooklyn Bridge if I thought that would turn them on. I was addicted to them as much as I was addicted to alcohol. I could not live without them.

Our next stop was Windsor, Ontario, where we took on another girl named Kay and continued to live it up. We were sleeping in Windsor and working in Detroit. The girls found out that they could make a lot of money in Detroit and all I had to do was sit in a bar and wait for them to make enough money for us to have a party. We had some wild times in Windsor and Detroit, but eventually had to leave—we were asked to leave each and every hotel because of the wild parties we threw and the police were getting fed up with us. We were all sorry to leave Windsor but nothing really changed in our lifestyle, just the scenery.

Next stop, Sault Ste-Marie. After only two days there we were told to leave town by the police. This was the only place in our travels where we actually got an escort out of town. We headed into northern Ontario, where we had to cool our act a little because the people went to bed around midnight and there was little else to do but join them.

I got some bad news on our first stop, which was Hearst, Ontario. Dale went to see a doctor and was told that she was pregnant. This, if anything, made us drink more. Again, I began to notice strange things happening to me. The girls would tell me of the things I did the night before, but I was having blackouts and could not remember doing them. I seemed to be getting meaner when I drank, and I was always looking for a fight. I was really hooked on alcohol at this time and could not live without it. I wanted more and more.

We continued our trip through Northern Ontario, to Kapuskasing, Port Arthur, and Fort William, until we arrived in Winnipeg, Doris' hometown. Her mom and dad lived there and they tried in vain to talk her into staying home and getting a job, but she wouldn't so they grudgingly gave her their blessings. At the time, I was afraid that Doris would decide to stay home, but I soon wished she would have, because at our next stop she told me that she also was pregnant!

I remember being very discouraged and worried about these new circumstances, and this made me drink all the more. I dreaded any kind of responsibility and could not handle it. Whenever I had a problem and wanted to get rid of it, I solved it by getting drunk even though the next morning was worse.

I believe that Doris' pregnancy was a threat to what little security I had and as a result, my hostility when I drank increased until I actually assaulted Dale during one of my blackouts, giving her a black eye. We were in Regina, where Doris had lived before, and she remembered a couple of girlfriends that she used to go out with. She invited them up to the hotel.

One of them was a beautiful girl named Eileen. I could not take my eyes off her. We drank a lot that night, and when it came time for Eileen to go home I insisted on taking her. We went by way of a big park, and it was there that I talked her into sitting down to rest. I made love to her. She was beautiful, and a girl I will always remember.

When I got back to the hotel, Doris was in

Dale's room. I knocked on Dale's door and asked Doris to come back to our room. She said she wanted to sleep with Dale. I was furious, and cursed them, then went back to my room and continued to drink until I passed out.

In the morning I found out that I had assaulted Dale by punching her in the eye. She threatened to go to the police, which gave me cause to run away again. I was beginning to form a pattern. Whenever I got myself into trouble, or if I had to accept responsibility, I would get lost. I could not look after myself properly. How was I supposed to look after Doris and her baby? I had repeated what happened with Dale.

There was a carnival not too far away and I ran there. The carnival was Wallace Brothers Shows; operated and owned by Pat and Jimmy Sullivan. They gave me a job on the Pie Car, where I looked after the bar from midnight until eight A.M. There were all-night poker games where I served the players drinks, sandwiches, and coffee. I liked this job and got to know everyone on the show pretty fast, especially the girls who were working the girlie shows. There was one car just for the girls, which was right next to the Pie Car and was out-of-bounds to nearly everyone but me. If any of the girls wanted to get up early, they would leave their names and berth number on the blackboard behind the bar and I would wake them up.

There was one little dancer called Betty, who always wanted to help me behind the bar. I doubt if she was five feet tall, and we were both in heat all of the time. She loved variety in her sex life, just as I did, and there were some very embarrassing moments. For example, I would be talking to a customer at the bar and she would be doing things to me that should only be done in bed and in private. I would try to talk intelligently and keep a straight face, but I could not always control myself. One moment my customer would be talking seriously, and suddenly I would blurt out, "Oh God! Oh! Oh! Oh! Oh!" The customer would look at me with a puzzled look and say, "Are you all right?" I would answer, "Oh, it's just a cramp," or, "I feel sick," and head for the washroom. Betty, I am sure, got an extra lift from my discomfort, because she seemed to pick the oddest times to be around me, and she liked making me squirm.

On the show they seemed to frown on people who were pill-poppers, but they couldn't care less if you smoked pot. I believe I was oversexed to begin with, but when I smoked a joint of marijuana, sex seemed to last longer and feel better. It was an aphrodisiac that elevated me to a new high in sexual feelings. I didn't know why I could never be satisfied with my natural feelings but I realized that the more satisfaction I got, the more I wanted.

About this time I met a young guy about the same age as myself by the name of Pat Crosby. He was working as a shill for a couple of concession-aires, and he kept me company when I was working the bar at night. We got along well and soon were going out on double-dates; we traded information and compared the girls we went out with, sometimes even switching partners after get-ting what we wanted. Pat and I had a lot in common, and we both had an insatiable appetite for sex.

When the shows were concluded, the carnival was torn down and transported to a new location. This was always a time of great excitement and joy. Most "carnie" people are gypsies and drifters, as I was, and we believed that all our dreams would come true in the next town or at the next stop.

My drinking and pill-popping began to make me paranoid and fearful that everyone knew of my dependence on alcohol and drugs. But as soon as I arrived at a new site, I would look up a doctor and tell him of my "problems." If I wanted bennys, I'd tell him that I was falling asleep all the time and needed something to keep me awake. Often on the same visit to the doctor I would convince him that Benzedrine pills did such a good job at keeping me awake that I needed something to put me to sleep. I'd con him into giving me a prescription for Nembutal as well. I was too good at conning.

CHAPTER SEVEN

THE LOST YEARS

I got back into the magazine subscription business, this time with Pat from the carnival. Our next stop was back in Regina where Pat and I decided to hire some girls and start another crew. We checked into a hotel, placed an ad in the paper, and started interviewing girls.

Pat introduced me to Marie and I knew as soon as I saw her that I had to have her. Marie was only seventeen years old and her folks lived in Prince Albert, Saskatchewan. She had run away from home and landed in Regina about the same time we arrived there. Her mother was of German descent and her father was a full-blooded Indian. She had long black hair, a golden complexion and one of the most beautiful faces I had ever seen. I conned Pat into leaving the hotel and going on an errand. He was no sooner out the door than we were in bed together. Poor Pat, he came back looking for his girl and found her in bed with me.

After a couple of drinks I asked him if he wanted to join us in bed, maybe because I had a guilty conscience. He did, but Marie and I were so absorbed in each other that we completely ignored him and he finally got the message and went to his own room. I felt bad for a while, but I thought, all is fair in love and war, and I justified my actions by assuring myself that this was the real thing. I was sure I had found the right girl.

One of the other girls we had hired was Linda. She had some experience selling magazines so I just had to teach her the new sales pitch for nurse's training. Linda caught on fast and trained another girl named Hilda. I kept asking Marie to work with Linda so that she could get trained properly at selling magazines, but Marie kept telling me that she did not need any training; I had to agree with her because she was bringing in as much money as Linda and Hilda together. Another pleasant surprise I got was that Marie was giving me all the money she made. I offered her fifty percent but she insisted that I should look after the money. How could I argue with that? She was full of surprises, and I loved her.

We moved on to Saskatoon, where Marie kept bringing in more and more money. One night she arrived back at the hotel with a beautiful diamond ring, an expensive set of luggage and six hundred dollars. I asked her where she got it and she told me that she had met this fellow who wanted to marry her, and, knowing that we would be leaving town soon, she thought it would be a good idea to lead him on and let him think that she loved him so that she could get as much as she could out of him. I didn't object, but I worried a little because I thought that when this guy found out that she was conning him he might go to the police. I didn't want any heat. Also, we were making all the money we needed without running any risks, so why take chances? Anyway, it was too late to undo what she had done.

The diamond ring was meant to be an engagement ring, and he wanted the wedding to take place as soon as possible so that she would not change her mind. She saw him about twice a week and each time she came back with more gifts and money. I happened to look through one of her order pads and was really surprised to see that all her subscriptions were for twenty or twenty-five dollars, and that all her customers were living in hotels. This was why she was making more money than the other girls. She was getting laid with each subscription, and, knowing Marie, she must have loved her work.

Now that I knew what Marie was up to, I became nervous and irritable and of course my solution for this was to find a doctor and get some pills. I don't remember what the pills were but they sure had a dramatic effect on me. All I remember is that I woke up in a jail cell in police headquarters in Saskatoon, charged with indecent assault.

Here I was, twenty-one years of age. I had a criminal record for breaking and entering and assorted offences, and now indecent assault. Believe me, this could not possibly have happened if I were in my right mind. I needed a girl like I needed a hole in my head. Marie was more than enough to fill all my sexual needs and I was also getting some from Hilda. They both said that I had brought a girl up to my hotel, given her something to drink, and then tried to get into her pants, but she had objected. I then offered to walk her home, and it was on the way home, when we were walking through the park, that I had assaulted her.

She had some marks on her throat where she claimed that I tried to choke her and her clothes were torn, so the police knew she was telling the truth. I knew that I was telling the truth when I told them that I did not know who assaulted her, and that I certainly had not. This may sound like bull-shit to people who have never experienced a blackout, but I had been in a blackout, and only people who have experienced them know that you can't remember a thing. I felt so terrible when I realized that I must be guilty.

All this happened in late October, and I was sent to the provincial jail in Prince Albert, Saskatchewan, about one hundred miles away, to await my trial. I asked Pat to get me a good lawyer and he got me the best. His name was Emmett Hall, and he later became Chief Justice of the Supreme Court of Canada. Pat and the girls took off in different directions; I didn't expect to see them again. I was on a real downer when I arrived at this dreary prison on the outskirts of this town where I did not know anybody.

My first impression of the jail was bad and my indoctrination into its system and rules did not go too smoothly. After I had changed my clothes to prison garb, they took me to a section of the prison where I was placed in a cell among other prisoners who were also awaiting trial. I must admit the cell was clean enough, but as I looked around I had a foreboding of bad luck. I was thousands of miles from home, in a strange town, a strange prison, a strange cell, and nothing but strangers all around me. As I look back I think that was one of the loneliest nights of my life— and probably the saddest.

I am glad to say that first impressions are often wrong and feelings can change pretty quickly. I had gotten over my alcohol and drug withdrawal symptoms at police headquarters in Saskatoon, and by the time I got to this jail I was in pretty good shape physically. Fortunately, I had never had any trouble making friends. I have always liked the old saying that strangers are only friends you haven't met yet. It wasn't long before I became one of the boys and was accepted as a bona fide member of the prison population. I found out pretty quickly what was going on and who had the right connections; prison life got much easier.

As I said earlier, Pat and the girls took off in all directions after I was arrested, so you can imagine my surprise when a guard came to my cell and told me to get ready for a visitor. I thought for sure there was a mistake so imagine my surprise when I saw my beautiful Marie. I couldn't believe my eyes, and I don't think I was ever so happy to see anyone.

Marie had been at court a couple of times but they had not let me see her alone so I didn't get to talk to her. Later I tried to explain to her, but I wasn't too sure myself what had happened. I would have to await my trial to get all the facts. She was very understanding and told me that she still loved me. She was staying with her parents in Prince Albert, and said that she would try to get up to see me every day. Doing time was a lot easier with Marie coming up all the time. If I remember correctly, inmates awaiting trial could get visits anytime. Marie was a regular visitor, and I am sure that the other prisoners envied me because Marie brought cartons of cigarettes, fruit, candy, and boxes of chocolate—everything a guy could want. She was a godsend and I loved her.

I did not know what the date of my trial was. My lawyer told me that I would be going to high court (Court of King's Bench) sometime before Christmas, but he would not give me a date. I just had to hope that when I did go, I would be freed. Finally, I got word that my trial would be the twenty-second of December, three months after I had been arrested. The day arrived, and everyone who had told me that my lawyer was the best and that I could not get much time if I were convicted, proved to be right. I was convicted and given a sentence of one day in jail, to be served at the RCMP headquarters in Saskatoon. I was to be set free on the twenty-third of December, two days before Christmas.

As soon as I was released, I headed back to Prince Albert, where I checked into the Marlborough Hotel, which was a nice place, especially after being where I had been. I called Marie, she came right down and we had a wonderful Christmas together. I had Christmas dinner at her home. She had saved some money while I was away, so we got in a supply of liquor and had a ball.

At that time, and for many years to come, I could not conceive a good time without a supply of liquor, some grass, or a supply of pills, especially bennys, which enabled me to drink longer, sober up faster, and relieve the ever-present hangover. Although I was unable to get the pills I wanted in Prince Albert, we succeeded in getting high on sex, booze, and grass.

After the holidays, Marie and I went out hustling. We still had the magazine order pads, and we did well, but I could not get used to the cold in Prince Albert, where it reached fifty below zero, so we headed for warmer places. The first town we hit was Regina, Saskatchewan, and oh, how I wished we had gone somewhere else! I had always had bad luck there and this time was no exception.

We checked into a hotel and began getting ready for bed. Marie was in the bathtub when we were both startled to hear a loud banging on the door, followed by two big dummies who came charging into the room with guns drawn, yelling at us to get against the wall with our hands up and not to make any wrong moves or they would blow our heads off. Talk about Keystone Cops. I guess they were short of criminals in Regina. These two were pretty desperate for any kind of arrest, and they pounced on us as if we were Bonnie and Clyde. They questioned us about every theft or robbery that had happened for the last couple of years.

Finally, after what seemed like hours of questioning, they allowed us to get dressed and took us down to police headquarters. I think they finally charged me with contributing to juvenile delinquency, because Marie was only seventeen. The next morning I appeared before a judge who turned Marie over to some social workers and sent her home to Prince Albert, and ordered me to not see her again. It would be twenty-five years before I saw her again.

I was really heartbroken to see Marie go, and I cursed the judge and the cops and their ideas of justice. I also knew that if I had had the money to hire a high-priced lawyer, and could have afforded to have Marie's parents come to court to testify that they had given their consent for us to stay together until we had the money to get married, then justice would have been different for us. I have experienced two kinds of justice in our great system—you will get justice if you have the money, and will get shit if you are broke. The State balanced the books by letting the rich go free and sending the poor to jail. Of all the jails I have been in I have yet to meet a rich man.

In Edmonton I changed my approach to selling subscriptions. In the past I had gone door-to-door; now I had the bright idea of standing on the corner and picking my customers. Most of my door-to-door sales were to young single women or young wives, so I reasoned that if I did not have to waste time with older people, I could make more money. I took up a position on a very busy corner across from the hotel, and started picking my customers. When I saw a good prospect approaching I stepped out in front of her and said, "Pardon me, miss, my name is Pat Murphy," or whatever name I was using, and asked her to support me by signing my petition.

I improved my sales pitch to the point where I very seldom got turned down, and sometimes,

after selling some of them, I even conned them up
to my hotel room and out of their pants. There was
always some liquor in my room, and after a few
drinks I broke down their defences, sometimes
staying in bed with them for a couple of days. In
my mind this was really living. I could not imagine anyone having a better job than mine.

Not knowing that I was poisoning myself, I
believed that to be happy you needed three ingredients: wine, women and song. To that I added a
fourth ingredient: drugs. I could get high on sex or
booze or drugs, and sometimes had a hard time
choosing what type of a high to go after. Each time
I tried to surpass the last high. I remember having
sex after using amphetamines or bennys and thinking that I was going to blow my mind. There were
times when the rumbling seemed to start in my
groin and crawl slowly up my body to my brain,
eventually driving me to the brink of insanity.
Often, I actually screamed in the heat of passion,
being so unable to control myself that I ended up
scaring the hell out of the girl. At the time, I
thought that everyone screamed when they reached
a climax. I also went to extremes in other ways. If
a movie was sad I was not able to control my tears;
if it was funny I laughed until my sides ached. It
was obvious I had grave emotional problems.

The only relief that I got from my sexual feelings was when I was spaced out on drugs or booze. I could sympathize with those poor bastards who got sent to jail for rape. There, I thought, but for the grace of God, go I. The only difference between them and me was that I could pick up a girl and usually get her into bed. But I was afraid that I was capable of rape, and dreaded the thought that someday I might go that far.

I had been in Edmonton a month or so and had made some friends who were heavy drinkers like myself, and who did not mind an odd joint or benny to give them a further lift. Some nights we ended up at the home of one of the couples, and continued the party there. There were a lot of bootleggers in Edmonton, as I recall, and we had no trouble replenishing our liquor supply.

It was at one of these parties that something happened that was to change my life. We had been having a real good time for a couple of days. We had run out of booze two or three times. Someone had always volunteered to go to the liquor store for more, but this particular time we decided to cut the cards—the high card would go. I drew the high card, and I remember having to hurry because the liquor store was to close within a half-hour, and they were afraid I would not make it in time. I called a taxi and got there before it closed.

Upon leaving the liquor store I walked to the intersection to hail a cab, when I noticed a very pretty girl coming towards me. She said, "Hello, Earl," which really surprised me. Then I realized that it was Doris, whom I had abandoned the year before when she was pregnant. I had not known that she was in Edmonton, and she certainly did not know that I was there, so we were both taken completely by surprise. I asked her if she would come up to my hotel for a drink, and she accepted, so I never got back to the party. I think we stayed in bed for three days, only getting up when we had to eat or go to the washroom. We started right back where we had left off the year before. I inquired about the baby and she said he was healthy and very happy. A farm couple in Saskatchewan was looking after him, and Doris was paying them so much a month.

Doris and I got back together, and it was not long before she was pregnant again. I was shocked and my first thought was to get the hell out of there. As usual I wanted to run when I felt there was trouble, and until now I always had, but I really cared for Doris. I cannot say that it was love, because that was something that I did not understand, but I liked her company and she filled my need for sex, so I decided to at least stick around a while longer.

She must have known what I had in mind because she wrote a long letter to my Mother. A short time later I received a letter from home, in which my Mother advised me that the only decent thing to do was to marry Doris and make a home for her and the kids. I am convinced that this is the only bad advice that my Mother ever gave me, but she, of course, had no way of knowing how insane I had become or the monster I would turn into.

We soon left Edmonton and moved to Winnipeg, where Doris' parents were living. They had a large house and they rented a couple of rooms. They had an empty room when we arrived, but her old man was an Englishman from the old country, and very strict, and although we told him that we were getting married, he would not accept us living together until after the wedding. Doris was to sleep downstairs and I was to sleep upstairs. Her father was a strange little character. He was always pulling practical jokes and acting like a frustrated comedian. He kept a close watch on us, but every morning, Doris came up to my room carrying a broom to look as though she was just cleaning my room, but as soon as she entered she put down the broom and we would do the natural thing.

There was a young couple living directly across the hall from me, and one morning, when the husband had gone to work and his wife was home, I experienced one of my most embarrassing moments. Poor Doris. It must have been worse for her. There I was on top of her, exercising my rights and trying to keep my passion under control and my growling down, when suddenly the door was burst open by a wild Indian man, who began screaming and jumping up and down. He was in full dress with war paint and feathers, and, to make matters worse, he had let the girl across the hall in on his little joke; she was standing in the doorway, with a strange expression on her face. Doris and I jumped out of bed, very naked and very shocked.

The frustrated comedian, when he got his composure back, ordered us out of his house, never to return. I was glad to leave; it was too quiet around there. But I think it took a long while for Doris to get over it, because she loved her father. We left Winnipeg, and she never saw her father again. We soon arrived in Montreal and Doris had our second child. I was glad to be back home, but things only got worse.

I started drinking more, smoking pot and occasionally shooting up, but I was determined to stay away from heroin, morphine, and other hard drugs. I was convinced that the lesser of the evils was alcohol and I was certain that alcohol would do the least damage, so I proceeded, unknowingly, to destroy myself. What I did not realize was that alcohol was cunning, baffling, and powerful, and that it would take me to places I did not want to go, and make me do things that I did not want to do.

For the next twenty to twenty-five years I was in a semiconscious state, and I believe that I had two personalities. Like Jekyll and Hyde, one person yearned for decency, respectability, responsibility, to be a good father, husband, and good example to my kids. The other person was full of hate, had little or no conscience, was capable of anything—even murder—and with each drink became more rotten, terrorizing the people around him and acting like the devil himself.

I can remember so well the agony of waking up in the morning and hearing about the atrocities that I had committed the night before, all the while knowing that I had to be completely insane to have done those things. And yet, I could not stop drinking. I began to hate myself with a passion, and I tried to self-destruct. I was always looking for the toughest and strongest guys to fight.

I remember one guy who was known as a good

boxer. He was fighting out of New York and Boston. His name was Gussie Mell, and I became obsessed with the idea that I had to find him and beat him to prove to everyone that I was a better boxer than he was. I did find him a few times, unfortunately for me, and we did have a few fights, but I am sure that I never came close to winning any of them. I didn't know that poor old Gus had the same disease that I had—alcoholism.

We eventually became good friends, even partners for a while selling punch boards. We had five, ten and twenty-five cent boards. The twenty-five cent boards had a thousand punches and were small and compact enough to fit in a waiter's pocket, so we sold them to waiters in the beer parlours and clubs in downtown Montreal. We paid about eighteen dollars a dozen for the boards and sold them for seven dollars each. They brought in two hundred and fifty dollars and paid out a hundred. There were four prizes of twenty-five dollars each. We knew where the winners were, and if Gussie sold a board to a waiter, I went in later and punched out a winner. If I sold the board, Gus went in and did the same. We were making a good dollar; except that when you are drinking you cannot hold on to money, so the more we made, the more we spent.

I can well imagine the suffering and shame that Doris went through because of me. I would arrive home at three o'clock in the morning, the Great Lord of the Manor, demanding that she get the hell out of bed and make me something to eat, and poor Doris would comply, partly to stop me from yelling and scaring the kids, but also because she did not want to move again. We seemed to be forever looking for a new place to live. I cannot remember too much about this period, only that I was shooting up a lot, popping pills, and drinking.

I had a buddy around this time who was a heavy drinker, but not a drug user. Matt was big, at least two hundred and fifty pounds, and when we drank together I could never predict what might happen. At first our escapades were not too bad. We would mug some drunk, or pick up a couple of girls and end up in a motel having a party, but after a while our actions got more and more insane. Matt was an embalmer by trade, and he had a half-interest in a funeral parlour. With the work he had to do, it was easy for me to understand why he needed a drink to relax.

It was funny how we met. I had been sitting in a club with my brother Bob and a couple of other guys, drinking. My brother was a big man, six foot three, two hundred and forty pounds. A jerk at the

next table began insulting him. I could not understand how he could just sit there and take it, but
my brother did not like fighting. I was ashamed of
him and thought he was yellow. Because I happened to love fighting I began insulting the guy
back. It did not take long for all hell to break loose.
Whenever I fought a guy I thought was too strong
for me I would always try to find an equalizer. I
was in the habit of carrying a switchblade, a lead
pipe, or some similar type of weapon, but on this
night I had nothing, so I had to improvise. There
were a few quarts of beer on the table, which I
grabbed and started throwing at him. The customers headed for the doors. In the end we all
became friends and Matt and I became good bud-
dies. We both loved trouble and we were to get
plenty of it.

God knows I tried often enough, but a big reason for my drinking was what I felt a drink did for
me. I was normally a shy, quiet person who could
not talk to girls and had a deep inferiority com-
plex. I was also full of fears, but as soon as I took
a drink I became about ten feet tall, could talk to
anyone, and conquered all my fears. Alcohol
transformed me from a mouse into a tiger, and I
thought this transition was great, until I finally
realized the harm that I was doing to myself, and

my friends and loved ones.

I began to hate myself and I spread my hate to my wife and kids and everyone else around me. I lived to drink and get high on drugs. I could not realize the extent of the damage that alcohol and drugs were having on my mind and body and so I blamed my troubles on everything but alcohol. I started to lose days and weeks, not remembering what happened. I could not do anything without a drink, and after a few drinks was just as useless. My actions were becoming more and more insane.

One night my buddy, Matt, and I were in a downtown nightclub when I got into a fight with a waiter. We started breaking tables and chairs and throwing everything we could get our hands on at the bar. We were really wrecking the place. Someone called the police, and on our way out we passed the police on the stairs as they were coming in. "Hurry up," I yelled at them, "someone is wrecking the joint!"

As they rushed into the club we spotted the keys in the ignition of their police car. We jumped in and took off with the siren blaring. Someone ran in and told them that their car had been stolen. They came out, commandeered a taxi and chased us across town. They emptied their guns shooting at us. Finally, other police cars took up the chase and we were cornered and arrested. Matt was grazed by a bullet that creased his skull—the hair has never grown back. I ended up with a split knee and a face full of shattered windshield glass. After being patched up I was sent to Bordeaux Jail, where I remained for nearly three months awaiting trial on a charge of car theft. I spent the time picking glass out of my face, and considering myself lucky that I wasn't blind.

Matt had no police record and his folks were well-to-do. We got a good lawyer who was able to get the fix in. The lawyer told me that I would have to spend a little time in the trial ward at Bordeaux because of my record, but that when we came to court the case would be thrown out. Matt got out on bail right away. I really trusted the lawyer we had. He was recognized as one of the best fixers in Montreal.

One Saturday morning, they took me from my cell and told me I was going to court. I told them they were making a mistake, that my court appearance was July seventeenth and that this was only the eighth but they said they had orders to take me to court, so that was where I was going. I didn't mind because it got me a day out of my cell anyway.

When I got to the courthouse I was held with

some other prisoners in the bullpen, and after a short wait they called my name and proceeded to take me downstairs to the judge's private chambers. When I walked in everyone was laughing and joking. The two cops were there, the prosecutor, the clerk of the court, our lawyer, Matt and the Judge. After a few minutes they called the court to order and the prosecutor read the charges: car theft, damaging property, avoiding arrest. We had been advised to plead not guilty, and we did so; then the judge took over. He talked for a few minutes and then concluded by saying, "Next time you take a car, take your lawyer's—he has a lot more money than the police." He apparently thought this to be a great joke, and so we all laughed and he dismissed the case and suggested that I attend the forensic clinic at the Allan Memorial Hospital in Montreal (a mental hospital).

It was about this time that I became very concerned about my behaviour, and went to see a doctor. I was hoping that he would tell me why I acted the way I did, but all I got was more pills. That seems to be the cure-all for people with mental and emotional problems. Instead of help, the good doctor just increased my problems. Soon I was like a zombie. I was in a daze most of the time and my wife was afraid to leave me alone with the kids because I would keep falling asleep with a cigarette in my hand.

I finally began to realize that I had a very serious mental problem. When I was sober I got along fine with everyone, but as soon as I took a drink no one knew what would happen, including me. And I was scared because I knew that I was capable of murder; I was especially afraid that I might kill my wife or one of my kids.

So, again, I tried to find help and was referred to the forensic clinic, where they gave me Valium, Librium, and other assorted pills. If you think I was confused before, you should have met me after a couple of months of their "treatment." I soon had a medicine cabinet that rated with the best. I brought some of my new-found friends from the clinic over to compare pills—Darvon, Largactil, Phenobarb, sleeping pills, wake-up pills, all sorts of tranquilizers. The hospitals and clinics were bent on relieving my problems by destroying what little of my brain I had left. I became a statistic.

I refer to this period of my life as "The Semiconscious Years." I had my suspicions that we patients were being used as guinea pigs. We were given certain pills for a month or so, after which they brought us in and questioned us about the effects the pills had on us. In my case, the staff had my wife come in to explain how I was behaving at home, and to confirm if the pills had produced a change in my behaviour. When I first attended this clinic, I was hopeful that they would help me become aware of my problems and perhaps find a solution to them. But the end result was that the longer I attended their clinic, the more insane I became, until eventually I was committed to a mental hospital, where I felt right at home. The few sessions that I had had with the psychiatrists at the forensic clinic should have prepared me for what was to come.

I had a low opinion of these treatments, which consisted of pills, pills, and more pills. I also did not think too much of the shrinks, although I was a little jealous of them because I thought they were keeping the best pills for themselves, but I couldn't relate to them. They came from the side of the tracks where I stole my bread and milk. They had never suffered hunger pains, or been beaten within an inch of their lives. They had never tasted the loneliness, the fears and frustrations, the bitterness and depressions. How many of them had woken up in a freight car half–frozen to death on a January morning, hardly able to walk? They had no experience of being caged like an animal, and they had never survived on pure, unadulterated hate. Yet they claimed to know how I felt! When I realized the distance between what I thought were my problems and what they thought were my problems, I began to lose hope.

Then an opportunity arrived in the person of Dr. Dormier. I had been told quite often what a great and important man he was, and how to conduct myself in his presence. I was determined to level with Dr. Dormier, and be as honest as I could because I really believed that he could help me. As I waited in his outer office, and the time came and went for my appointment, I thought he had forgotten all about me. But I was assured by his secretary that he would be seeing me, and that I must understand that he was a busy man. Finally, after waiting nearly an hour past my appointment time, I was ushered into his private chambers.

The room was quite dark, and it took a few moments for my eyes to adjust. At first I thought I was alone, but then I noticed a very large desk. I was shocked to see a person's head peeking above the desk. My first impression was that there was a kid behind the desk, but then I remembered that kids don't have bald heads. I had pictured him in my mind and thought that he would be a big, important-looking man. Another thought crossed my mind, that maybe they were playing a practical joke on me, but then I heard his voice, and there was no mistake. The voice was gruff and authoritative, as though it was coming from someone who thought they were important.

He told me to sit down and then asked me to talk about myself. I gave him a run-down of my past and what I was doing now. I remember talking fast because I thought he would terminate the interview at any moment. When I had my appointment with Dr. Dormier, I was deeply involved in a swindle at a few department stores downtown. I had this swindle so well organized that I could make as much money as I wanted. As sick as I was, I knew that I needed help, and so I decided to level with the doctor. I had enough common sense to realize that if I didn't tell him the truth, there wouldn't be much hope for my going straight; so I told him everything that I thought he should know.

The week after my appointment, my wife had her appointment with him; I remember how disappointed she was when she returned. The first thing he had asked her was if she knew that I was a pathological liar. She answered no, and then he gave her a run-down of the things I had told him. She told me that she had interrupted him to say that I had not been lying—that what I had told him was the truth. From that day on I lost all faith in shrinks, and never took them seriously again.

The forensic clinic was a section of the Allan Memorial Hospital, which the CIA had used for experiments on people, without first getting their permission. These patients had been heavily sedated with LSD and many other drugs to find out what the effects were. They found out years later that Dr. Cameron, who was in charge of the hospital, and the CIA were working together, and that the CIA was funding the experiments, using the patients as guinea pigs. I recall being sent to the Allan for tests and treatment at different intervals and being kept for short periods of time. But in my drugged condition I would never have known whether I was one of the guinea pigs or not. What I do know is that my mental condition worsened; thank God that I got out of their clutches and escaped further treatment.

I was sent to the Douglas Hospital, a hospital for the insane, where there was a section for treating alcoholism, but their solution to alcoholism was to change your addiction from alcohol to drugs. I became so spaced-out on their steady diet of pills that I could not distinguish one day from the other. I lost all interest in sex, in girls, and, in fact, in living. I had been considered a violent person on the street; in here, I was turned into a kitten. I heard from other patients that our food was loaded with saltpetre, which explained why there were no sex problems. Even though the women and men were together, the drugs they gave me made me so docile that I turned into a pussycat!

I am sure they saved a lot of money on staff, because we were so dazed and tired all the time that we did not have the energy to argue or to care what they were doing to us. We received our small plastic container with our pills every few hours, and the nurse made sure we swallowed them. The staff called us into their offices to write out progress reports while knowing that the drugs being prescribed were killing our brains, asked questions and expected us to give intelligent answers. Most of the time I did not even know where I was, or who I was. The only feeling I had left was a feeling of hopelessness. I could not cry or laugh or sing or enjoy anything. I couldn't even remember if I was depressed. When you can't think I guess you can't feel. Years later I read a pamphlet put out by a group of doctors in Alcoholics Anonymous, which stated that drugs destroy the brain faster than alcohol. I can certainly agree with them.

These doctors had to know that they were

destroying our brains, the only thing that could get us well. We saw patients arrive there sick and confused, and watched as they grew more sick and more confused. If he or she showed any anger or argued with the staff, then the dosage was increased to the point where the drugs extinguished what little spark of life was left, and eliminated the patients' chances of ever having a normal life.

Years later when I became a therapist, I received a phone call one night from a woman who told me that she had been drinking and had taken an overdose of pills. Her husband had died recently, and she felt that she could not live without him. She thought she would be better off dead. As we spoke, I noticed a change in her voice, and then suddenly there was no sound at all. I dressed hurriedly, ran out to find a cab and proceeded to her home. She lived in a high-rise, and when there was no answer to my ringing, I located the janitor and explained my concern to him. He got a passkey and we went to her apartment where we found her lying on the sofa, unconscious. We tried to revive her, without success. We called an ambulance, and it soon arrived, along with an emergency oxygen van from the fire department. They could not bring her around, so we finally rushed her to the hospital, where she remained in a coma for six hours. They pumped her stomach.

I will never forget that long, long night. It seemed like a week of waiting in the corridor outside the emergency room until finally the doctor informed me that she was out of the coma, and also out of danger. What a relief that news was. They kept her there until noon so that she could be seen by the psychiatrist. This was a Saturday and she was told to come back to the hospital on Monday. I was afraid to take her home so I took her to a motel for the weekend, feeding her chicken soup and trying to give her some strength and hope to face life. When Monday came I took her back to the hospital to see the doctor whom she had seen on Saturday. She was in his office no more than ten minutes. When she came out she had two prescriptions: one for Valium, the other for sleeping pills.

I was so damn mad that I grabbed the two prescriptions, ran into his office and told him he was nothing but a quack and a drug pusher. I told him that I had met drug pushers in beer parlours, pool rooms, and back alleys, all across the country, but that he was the worst bastard of them all because people trusted him and came to him for help. Doctors in their right minds, I told him, didn't prescribe Valium or sleeping pills to an alcoholic at any time, but especially not after the patient had overdosed and nearly died. I tore up the prescriptions and threw them in his face, and suggested that if he read up on Valium he would find out that, when mixed with alcohol, Valium is a deadly drug. This woman was an alcoholic who could not stop drinking, and another addiction would either kill her or take away whatever natural resources she might have left to fight her addiction. I have known people who have died as a result of this type of prescription; I nearly died myself. This particular woman did stop drinking with the A.A. program, and became a healthy and happy human being. Thank God she escaped from this type of treatment.

I also went to meetings in A.A. while I was being treated by doctors. I remember not drinking for periods of three and six months, and being so proud and telling people that I had been sober for six months, when in fact I did not know the meaning of sobriety. As long as I was taking mind-altering drugs I would never be sober but would continue to be frustrated and confused. In A.A. we can pick a sponsor. This is a member who tries to help you over the rough spots, one who will encourage you, and usually try to get you working through the Twelve Steps. I was fortunate to have had some really great sponsors, and I am sure they all left their mark on me, but I had been hustling marks for so long, and conning everybody I could, that my brain was loaded with scheming and conniving—I could not even think straight. When I attended an A.A. meeting and they talked about honesty or God, I often walked out and criticized them for not talking my language.

CHAPTER EIGHT

HITTING BOTTOM

Bad habits if not taken seriously will induce addictions and I became aware of related addictions I could not shake—lies, theft, excuses, self-pity, self-deception, anger, frustrations. My steady diet of alcohol and drugs was producing an individual who could not live with or understand himself.

Someone once gave me a book to read, hoping that it might help me. The book was *A Monkey On My Back*. The author was hooked on drugs, and I can well remember thinking at the time that he was lucky. I had a whole family of monkeys on my back and they were growing larger all the time. I could no longer sleep with the lights out. I would wake up screaming, punching at the air from terrible nightmares. The booze paralysed my brain and helped me to escape from total hopelessness.

The babies kept coming, and I continued to get into trouble and go to jail. By this time I had seven children. I was thirty-two years of age. I had an ulcer and was mentally sick with grave emotional problems. My anger often turned to rage, and I terrorized my children. I had come full circle, a chip off the old block. I had inherited my father's disease, and, oh, how I hated myself.

Then I was arrested yet again and charged with the hold-up of a taxi driver. The police put me in the trial ward at Bordeaux Prison, where I got in touch with a lawyer, Mr. Gagnon. I was lucky to be released on bail three weeks later. At the time I was really worried. I knew that, with my bad record, if I were convicted of this offence, I would be sent to a penitentiary for a long time.

I appeared in court for the first time for a voluntary statement, then a few weeks later for the preliminary enquiry. The lawyer wanted five hundred dollars before the trial. My poor darling Mom scrimped and saved and borrowed to pay the lawyer two hundred dollars. I tried in every way I could to get the three-hundred-dollar balance I owed the lawyer, but I couldn't raise it. The night before the trial I went to see the lawyer, and he told me that if I could not get the money before the trial the following morning, he would not appear in court to defend me. When he told me this, what little hope I had of beating the rap left me. For a while that night I thought seriously of packing a bag and running away, but after talking with Doris I decided to face the music.

What happened the following morning seemed strange at the time and I would think of it many times in years to come. Before Doris and I left for court, my Mom phoned to say she wanted to come with us. I tried to talk her out of it, but she was insistent, so we made arrangements to meet downtown. When we met I was sorry that she had come, because she was very pale, and looked sick. I knew she had been worrying all night.

As we continued our journey to the courthouse on the bus, I remembered her favourite phrase, "There is more wrought by prayer than this world dreams of." I watched her lips moving and knew that she was praying. We arrived at our destination, a square called Place d'Armes. My Mom was so pale that I worried that she might faint before we had covered the two remaining blocks to the courthouse. But when we had crossed the street we found ourselves directly in front of Notre Dame Cathedral, and a most amazing thing happened.

One moment my Mom was pale and worried, and the next moment her face broke out into the most beautiful smile I have ever seen, and she said that everything was going to be all right.

I looked at Doris and said, "My God, she's flipped, she's off her rocker!" and I began worrying more about her than my trial. I said, "Mom, please don't say things like that." She just continued to smile saying that everything was going to be all right. We finally arrived at the courthouse, where I turned myself in to the police because I was out on bail, and they put me in the bullpen.

I was the first one called that morning. I stood in the prisoner's dock and watched the courtroom come alive as the clerk of the court brought the jury members in. They took their places. There were some law students, the prosecutor, some police officers, witnesses and the general public who were interested in court cases. This was what people called High Court (Court of Queen's Bench), and the judge was the well-known judge, Wilfred Lazure, who handled mostly murder and other serious cases. He was honest and fair.

As he entered the courtroom everyone stood up; after he sat, everyone else sat. He had some words with the prosecutor, spoke to the clerk of the court, and, after seeing that everything was in order, he looked over at me and asked if I had a lawyer. I told him about my lawyer refusing to come unless I came up with the three-hundred-dollar balance. I was startled by the way the judge erupted on hearing this. He started yelling, questioning the ethics of a lawyer who takes a case through voluntary statement and preliminary enquiry, is there to help pick the jury, and then, for the most important day of all, the day of the trial, does not show up. I was very surprised at the judge's anger, and thought that I would suffer the consequences. To my horror he kept yelling about the lawyer, and threatened to notify the bar association. He finally calmed down and, looking over at me and said, "Never mind, I'll see that you are defended."

When the first witness was called, the prosecutor asked him a few questions. The judge apparently did not like his answers, so he asked a few questions also. The judge asked the witness how far away I was the first time he saw me. The witness said it was three o'clock in the morning and I was seventy-five to a hundred yards away. The judge told him he must have the eyes of an eagle to recognize a face from that far away in the dark. Then the witness told the judge that he could be wrong in his identification. The judge said that you cannot convict a man because you think it's him—you have to be one-hundred-percent sure.

The judge told him to leave the witness box, saying that he did not believe a word of the testimony. The witness looked so stunned that I almost burst out laughing.

The prosecutor called the second witness, who I am sure was so intimidated by the judge that, although he had identified me in the line-up at police headquarters, now thought he could have been mistaken. Then the two detectives were called, and the first detective got the same treatment as the first witness. The judge made both detectives look kind of silly, and I am sure that by this time they knew that their case had gone out the window.

In his summation to the jury, no lawyer could have done a better job than that judge did. I can still see the jurors nodding their heads in agreement with everything the judge said. I sometimes wonder if he enjoyed his role of defence lawyer that morning. The gist of it was that from all the testimony he had heard, there was too much doubt—the jury should not even leave the courtroom to consider the guilt or innocence of the accused and they should throw the case out. After his summation to the jury, and the jury agreeing to everything he said, he looked over at me and said, "Case dismissed. Don't you come back here again."

The events of that day will remain with me for the rest of my life, especially the beautiful smile that came to my Mother's face in front of the church when she told us with such conviction that everything would be all right. I'll always be sorry for doubting her.

I will never really know if I was guilty or not, because, like so many other times when I was arrested and charged with a crime, I had been in a blackout and could not remember what actually happened. One good thing about all this was that it made me more determined than ever to stop drinking, to get a job and to go straight.

Two or three weeks later I got a job on the railroad. It was the same railroad that I had worked on seventeen years earlier. Because my work record at that time was not a good one, and they had let me go, this time I changed my first name from Earl to Michael, and they hired me again. My salary was good, my ambition soared, I was working extra days and I was running all over the country.

I was a pretty good waiter and always made the most tips. I had been taught by some of the best waiters on the railroad, and in those days people took pride in their work. I always tried to recognize my customers' needs before they could ask for anything. If their water glass was half-full,

I filled it. I tried to provide the very best service, and, just before customers got up to leave, I told them what a real pleasure it had been to serve them, and that I hoped I could serve them again. I used all the little niceties to get a better tip, and it worked.

My Mom lived in a big house in downtown Montreal at this time, not too far from the railroad station, and after each trip I went to see her, both of us counting my tips on her bed, with her helping me. She was so happy and for the first time I felt proud of myself and started to gain a little self-worth. That summer was the best few months of my life, but it was not to last. I had been going to A.A. meetings and had not had a drink since April, I had a few hundred in the bank, my bills were paid, and I was in a state of ecstasy. Then, on the night of September 10, 1959, I came to know agony and suffering like I had never known before.

A friend of mine, Peter, who worked on the railroad with me, had rented a room from my Mom. He was waiting for me when I got off the train. His first words to me were "Mike, you have to come home right away." I guess I knew by the tone of his voice and the look on his face that it was something very serious. My first words to him were, "Is it Mom?" He would not tell me anything for the first few minutes in the taxi on the drive home, but I insisted that he tell me what happened, and he finally let me know that there had been a terrible accident and my family would tell me all about it at home.

When I got to the house everybody was crying and carrying on. My sister, Theresa, explained what had happened. Mom had gotten a phone call from a woman she knew who was pregnant and had a doctor's appointment. She told Mom that she would not be able to keep the appointment unless she got someone to mind her two other young kids. It was a Monday and although Mom was very busy she said she'd go.

Mom always did her washing on Monday along with a hundred-and-one other things. She always kept herself busy. One of her sayings was, "An idle mind is the devil's workshop." She was seventy-three years of age and worked like a young woman. She was always full of energy. When I went walking with her I could hardly keep up. Her biggest fault was that she didn't know how to say no, and people took advantage of her. Her family, including myself, had always taken advantage of her goodness, and even outsiders were taking advantage of her.

Mom was so innocent that she probably

thought God wanted her to help everyone. Theresa told me that Mom was run over and killed by a bus while rushing to keep the baby-sitting appointment. When I heard that I became sick and threw up, and cursed God for what he had done to her. I had got some faith I felt as a result of my court case, but I sure lost it in a hurry. I had always been anti-social, but now I became an anti-Christ, and all the old hatred and bitterness returned, only more so. I had a drink that first night after getting the news.

Then, as if to add to my sorrow and bitterness, the very next day I received in the mail a cheque for one thousand dollars from a twenty-year endowment policy that she had taken out twenty years earlier. I'll always remember how she scrimped and saved every penny to pay the premiums on her policies, often making do with the barest necessities so that she could provide us with a little nest egg for the future. She always thought of her kids. She was the most unselfish person I've ever known. I phoned my work, told them what had happened, and said that I would have to take a week off to make funeral arrangements and that I would be in touch with them later.

We had intended to have a simple funeral for Mom at the Joseph Wray Funeral Home in down-

town Montreal. We had rented a small room for
Mom. After I arrived at the funeral home, I looked
in all the small rooms and I remember how surprised I was when I could not find my Mother.
There was a large funeral service taking place at
the front of the building and I thought to myself,
as I pushed through the crowd, that it must be for
a celebrity. They had an enormous room and it was
packed with people. There were priests and nuns,
doctors and nurses, hookers, bums, every type of
person, and the crowd was getting bigger all the
time. I found my brother on the way out and mentioned to him that they had not laid Mom out yet.
He was surprised, and so we both headed for the
main office to see the funeral director.

We were in for another surprise. He told us
that one of the first people to arrive, upon seeing
Mom in the small room, had asked him to put her
in the large room. The stranger had promised to
handle any additional expenses, on one condition—that he remain anonymous. So poor darling
Mom, who had never caused a ripple or a wave in
her life, was finally being recognized and hon-
oured by all these people. My family and I were
flabbergasted by the turnout. The flowers were
coming in a steady stream, and so were the people.
The *Montreal Star*, our daily newspaper, ran many

ads in its memorial column promising to have masses for her. Beautiful poems were also published in memory of Mom Maloney.

I can well remember walking down the street with my Mother, and someone stopping us to greet my Mother with the words: "Dear Mom, how are you?" and these people giving her a hug and a kiss. I used to get pissed off, thinking, "What right do they have to call my Mother 'Mom'?" I was jealous. My heart was so full of hate in those days that I could not understand love—so how could I give it? I could not even show affection.

My Mom had been a nurse's aide at Queen Mary Veteran's Hospital for about ten years. She was supposed to retire at age sixty-five, as all government employees were required to. Well, when she reached that age they liked her so much that they fiddled the books so as to keep her three years longer. After the funeral I met one of the guests who had attended and asked him why he called my Mother "Mom." He told me a story I'll never forget. He had been a patient on a ward with a dozen or so men. One morning, just about dawn, Mom was collecting from the wards all the utensils that were to be sterilized. As she passed by his bed she noticed that he had "an accident" during the night. He was to be operated on because he could not control his bowels. This had happened to him once before and the other patients had never let him forget it. They razzed him every day. Mom left the ward with her utensils, and he was surprised to see her return about five minutes later. She pulled the curtain around the bed, cleaned him and the bed, brought clean sheets and left. He swore that she was not required to do this type of work, but she did not say a word. He thought this the most unselfish and kindliest act that he had ever experienced.

That patient said that no one on the ward ever learned that he had had an accident. Many years later I read that the true art of loving is to do something for someone and to never let anyone know about it. That was his reason for calling my Mother "Mom," and he added that the other patients had been calling her that long before he got there. My family and I had been receiving this kind of love from Mom all our lives but we took it for granted. In retrospect, when I think of the cards and presents that she received from as far away as Europe and Australia, I am sure that she left some love with many, many people.

Cyril took Mom's death the hardest. He only had one leg, and Mom had always taken extra good care of him, knowing that he needed her most. Although he was the oldest child, he had become dependent on Mom. Exactly two weeks to the day after my Mom died there was a knock at my bedroom door—my wife and kids were staying with me at Mom's place. To my surprise it was Cyril. He had not been around for a few days and we were all quite worried about him. He was pale, unshaven, and looked haggard. It broke my heart to see him this way. This was the guy who never forgot a joke, who was always capable of making people laugh but now it seemed that the life had gone out of him. He asked me if I had the price of a bottle of whiskey. I said, "Sure, Cy, get me one too."

When he returned with the whiskey we went downstairs to the kitchen, and as we drank we began to talk about Mom and he began to cry. We were both heartbroken. My wife and children soon joined us in the kitchen and I'll always remember that morning as the only time that Cy ever made us cry. I did not get the significance of his actions until it was too late. He held my children, hugging them tightly as the tears streamed down his face and he said his good-byes. Then it was my turn. We hugged for a few minutes but I don't remember anything that was said. I think we just cried. That afternoon my daughter Theresa looked into

Cyril's bedroom and saw Cy lying on the floor. It was only after I laid him on his bed that we noticed he was not breathing.

We called the police. My sister Mary, who had been one of eight applicants selected for the Montreal Police Force in 1947, took over when she arrived. There were two detectives from the morgue, also. They found a dozen or so Nembutals under his pillow and it was apparent to everyone that it was a suicide, but Mary somehow got the death report to read that he died of natural causes.

After Cy died, I tried to go back to work but my heart wasn't in it. My first night back on the train, the inspector caught me with my shirt collar open and my black bow tie hanging from the collar. I had been drinking, so I gave him a hard time and called him a lot of filthy names. He put me on report; after that I guess I was really too ashamed to go back.

After Mom and Cyril died I became very bitter. It was the year 1959. Nothing had ever affected me like this. I hated the world and everyone in it and I drew not one sober breath for at least a year. There were many times that I took enough pills to kill a horse but nothing worked. I often ended up on skid row, waking up in emergency rooms with broken bones or a split skull.

There was even one occasion when, having been hit over the head with a full quart of beer, the left side of my face was cut open. The intern made a bad job of stitching me up, and there were bumps every half-inch along the cut. I decided to play doctor and used my safety razor to smooth the surface of my face, ending up with a rather attractive dimple. I am sure a plastic surgeon could not have done a better job.

Although the black hole that I was digging for myself seemed to be getting deeper and deeper, every once in a while I would go back to A.A. Every time the meetings seemed to get worse, but something kept taking me back. I would arrive at precisely the time the meeting started and leave immediately when they ended. The chairperson would invite the people to stay for coffee and conversation but I could not get out fast enough. They had what they called "The Big Book," a book titled *Alcoholics Anonymous*, and another titled *Twelve Steps and Twelve Traditions*. They told us that it was very important for us to read them. My copies of these books gathered dust for many years.

Around this time I fell in with a gang of swindlers, or, as they called themselves, "fund-raisers." We bought sucker lists, or tap cards, with

the names of people who were in the habit of giving to good causes. We always tried to get good
sponsors, such as children with physical disabili-
ties, or retarded youngsters, or war veterans. We
invented sales pitches that made the sucker feel
obligated to give something. I remember compet-
ing with as many as a dozen con artists, each
trying to out-con the others. I knew that a con artist
was a professional liar, and that the best liar got
the most money. The fund-raisers paid you twenty
percent if you were a half-decent liar. When you
became more experienced and brought in more
than a hundred dollars a day, you could make
twenty-five percent and up. The sponsor ended up
with about ten percent and the organizer or promoter, after all expenses, usually got at least fifty
percent, which amounted to at least twenty-five
hundred to three thousand dollars a week.

The first "boiler room" I worked in was run by
a promoter who also owned a circus called Gartin
Bros. Circus. This guy really believed what
Barnum had said, that there was a sucker born
every minute. He would arrange with a disabled
children's hospital or another sponsor to provide
free tickets and buses to transport the children to
the circus. The sponsors usually thought that he
was a great guy for going to all this trouble for

their cause, but what they did not know was that he then called every company and business in the city, asking them to sponsor a bus load of fifty disabled children for a hundred bucks. Some companies sponsored four or five buses. I must admit that at first even I was a little naive, because I thought that we really were helping a lot of disabled children go to the circus but after several months of selling many thousands of tickets, I realized that there were not enough disabled children in the country to use the tickets I had sold. What really amazed me was to find out that there were so many gullible people.

My conscience must have bothered me, and I still get upset when I think of all the money that could have gone to the disabled children. At that particular time, unfortunately, I didn't care about anything but making money for my next drink. I cannot claim that I had any morals. Most of my fellow workers were also alcoholics, or had other serious hang-ups, and they couldn't care less about how they made their money.

We also had three or four collectors who rushed out to different sections of the city each morning with newly printed invoices. They returned at night loaded with cash and cheques. They received ten percent of the money that they brought in. We also got advances on the orders that were collected. Each night we anxiously awaited the return of the collectors so that we could get some drinking money. Most of the orders were sent through the mail, but the collectors of the remaining orders were making as much as one hundred dollars per day. The promoter of this scam made so much money with his boiler room that when his circus left town, he sent his brother to run it so that he could stay behind and promote other scams.

I began drinking like an alcoholic and for the next fifteen years was continually in a semiconscious state. My guilt, hate, shame and frustrations increased with each drink. The alcoholic always tries to find someone to blame and I blamed my wife and kids for my predicament.

I had been terrorizing my family in Montreal for the past few years, and whenever I stopped drinking I was full of remorse and self-hate. I had become exactly like my father; what I had always hated in him was coming out in me and I began to believe that someone had put a curse on me. Paranoia had set in and I was suspicious and distrustful of everyone. I had to sleep with the lights on; I believed my phone was tapped; I was certain that I was being followed. When I awoke in the night screaming from another nightmare, shaking with fear and sweat pouring off me, the only thing that helped was another drink.

At this point, I decided to leave Montreal and my family, and head for Vancouver, B.C. Although I would be three thousand miles away, I felt my kids would be better off without me. The year was 1970. I arrived there on a rainy day in November with good intentions. My plan was to straighten out my life once and for all and eventually return home to be a good father.

It rained every day for the next six months, and the loneliness I knew as a kid during my first year in reform school returned with a vengeance. Physical pain is nothing compared to the agony you go through when you lose everyone that you love. There were many times when I envied Cy, who was free from this agony of living. I only wished that I had the guts to follow his example. I attended Alcoholics Anonymous meetings and I got acquainted with some characters at the meetings who had stopped drinking but were still getting their kicks by popping pills or smoking up, usually grass or hash. They claimed to be sober, even accepted a cake for each year of their sobriety, but they had only switched their addiction from alcohol to drugs. At least my loneliness and remorse decreased to a bearable degree when I joined them.

I also claimed to be sober although at the time I didn't know what sober meant. My definition of sobriety kept changing and developing as I grew up and became more responsible, more stable, more mature. I am sure it means different things to different people. The people who defined the word for Webster's Dictionary could not have had a problem with alcohol or drugs—they could not have known the torment or the struggle or the years of hell that some alcoholics go through to attain sobriety. There are many who never make it. Many end up as "dry drunks"—they do not drink, but they remain resentful because they cannot, and they become the most miserable people you will ever meet. I was a dry drunk for years, until I found out how important it was to change my attitude, and to get grateful for my sobriety—but I am getting ahead of myself.

Another escape hatch of mine was to "fall in love," although I was a disaster for the women I became involved with. My ideas about how to treat a woman were very sick. As an inmate of different jails, you hear so much talk about how women like to be treated and what turns women on that some of this garbage sticks to you and you believe it. It took me years to unlearn a lot of this misinformation, and I came to the conclusion that the people who knew the least about love were the people who talked the most about it. I now know that what I felt was lust, not love. I had always been self destructive, and yet so many times in the depths of despair, and when I was suicidal, there came a woman who pulled me out of whatever hell I was in and gave me the will to survive a little longer.

I somehow got through that first year in Vancouver and on November 13, 1971, I had finally survived a year without a drink. I was so proud of myself when they called me up in front of my A.A. group and presented me with a one-year cake. My sponsor, Scotty, said a lot of nice things about me. I thanked the group for their support and told them how great it was to be sober. It was fifteen years since I had first walked through the doors of A.A. After receiving my cake that night a gang of us had a party. We popped pills, smoked up some grass and hash, and I discussed how good it was to be sober. It took me a few more years to realize that not drinking did not necessarily make me sober; it only made me more cunning.

In the fifth chapter of A.A.'s Big Book, they say that some alcoholics have grave emotional and mental disorders. I can relate to that. It also says that we have an alcoholic mentality— it was this mentality that allowed me to justify every rotten thing that I did. At the time I received my cake I had the following swindle going. I had met a copper miner at an A.A. meeting who was home on leave. We became good friends and I told him that I was about to open a new business, and that I was on the verge of signing a good deal with the local university to produce a winter carnival program. Now I had to sell my idea to someone who had some loot. This guy was made to order.

He hated his job as a miner, and when I told him that I was looking for a partner, and that, because he was so handsome and had such a terrific personality he would be the perfect partner, he agreed. Of course, I also told him that I could not accept just anyone as a partner. He had to have certain qualities, such as loyalty and trust. As an afterthought, I mentioned that he would also have to have at least five thousand dollars. The miner said that money would be no problem. He had saved a few thousand, and a finance company was always sending him letters asking if he needed any more money, because he was such a good customer in the past.

He came up with the money and shortly thereafter returned to the mines. As I diligently explained to him, there was no reason for both of us to be waiting for the deal to go through, so I strongly suggested that he go back to work and save his money in case we needed more. He promised to do better than that. He pointed out that he got free room and board at the mine, so he could send me his whole pay every two weeks. That was an offer I could not refuse, so I thanked him profusely and looked forward to his cheques every two weeks. One day he found me drunk and ended the deal. I thought I'd never see him again. When I started my recovery I found I couldn't forget this incident, and to improve the quality of my recovery I eventually paid him back the money I owed him.

It was not long after this that I went out and got drunk. I had been drinking for ten days or so, when a lovely young couple, Jim and Janet, also members of Alcoholics Anonymous, came to my rescue. They moved me out of the high-rise where I lived and took me home with them. It was only a matter of days before I fell madly "in love" with Janet, and I could hardly wait for Jim to leave in the morning so that we could make wild passionate love. I felt bad for betraying their trust, but I thought there were mitigating circumstances.

Right after Jim left for work in the morning, Janet would be out making my breakfast in a black see-through negligee that left nothing to the imagination. Not many men could have resisted the temptation. She wanted to run away with me but I decided to leave on my own.

Finding myself completely broke, I decided to try to score enough money at the welfare office for a room and some groceries. After waiting an hour or so, my name was called and I was ushered into a social worker's office. The woman was very pleasant. Her name was Betty, and it was not long before we were on a first-name basis. When I gave her a real hard-luck story, she seemed to sympathize with me and she got me a cheque for the balance of the month. She also got me some food vouchers and seemed so sorry for me that she soon had me believing that I was worse off than I thought.

I was so full of self-pity that I sat there thinking how great it was to find someone who understood. Betty even offered to drive me around as I hunted for a room or a bachelor apartment. While we drove around I got to know her a lot better. She was a divorcee with two sons, one had left home, and the other was still with her. I could not find a place that night, so she said that I could stay at her place. The next day I drove her to work and she said I could use the car, another offer I could not refuse. By this time I was thinking, why the hell should I look for a place when I could stay with her? I had gotten into the habit of using people, and although I was ignorant and had no real schooling, I had the gift of the gab and could manipulate people. For some strange reason people trusted me, even though I left a trail of disappointed, frustrated and injured people behind me.

Betty and I stayed together for a few months. Of course, I did not appreciate anything she had done for me—there wasn't a grateful bone in my body. In fact, I thought I had done her a favour. After each relationship scam that I pulled off, I came to hate myself a little more, and usually ended up getting drunk.

My next scam came while I was looking for a job. I was walking down one of the main streets when I saw signs in the windows for part-time help—waitresses, waiters, busboys, dishwashers. An idea began to form in my mind. I began to think that there must be many occasions in the hotel and restaurant industry—such as private parties, banquets, weddings—where management needed instant help. I spoke to a few restaurant owners and explained my idea. If a couple of waitresses did not show up for work on a very busy day, I asked, would it be worth one dollar an hour extra to be able to pick up the phone and get the replacements right away? I promised that my company would be able to replace anyone—cooks, bartenders, hostesses. Everyone I talked to agreed that it would be a great service, so all I needed was financial assistance.

I was so excited about my new idea that being broke did not bother me too much. I walked into a club and saw three guys sitting at a table. I was acquainted with one of them and I blurted out that I was about to open a new business, and that it was a gold mine. When one of the guys asked if I would like a partner, I played hard to get and told him about all the work that I had put into this project. The end result was that I sold him twenty-five percent for five thousand dollars. We closed the deal right there at the table with a handshake and seven hundred and fifty dollars cash. This was to show me that he was serious, and we made an appointment to meet at his lawyer's office the next morning to draw up the papers. The money he gave me to seal the deal allowed me to find an office, buy some secondhand furniture, order business cards and invoices, rent the phones, hire a girl, and place ads for part-time help.

I got a pleasant surprise with response to my ad. There were a lot of people on unemployment insurance who wanted to work two or three days a week and get paid under the table. I named the company Fast Action—Hotel and Restaurant Help When You Need It.

I soon realized that running the business was not what I wanted but I thought I could sell it off. I placed another ad in the business opportunities columns of newspapers, and caught a couple of live ones. To one, I sold a twenty-five percent share of the company, and to the second a fifty percent share. Altogether, I had owned the business one month. At the time, I wasn't stable enough to handle the pressure of running the business, but many years later I found out that this business really was a gold-mine and was still operating.

There were so many times when I would think that life could not get any worse, only to descend to new depths of horror, hopelessness and degradation. When I needed a fix, there was nothing too rotten or too low. I would do anything: steal a purse, climb through an open window of a house, grab something of value anywhere.

I was still associating with a lot of junkies and I started shooting and mainlining drugs again. I tried hard to control my intake, but after a while my intake began to control me. I became obsessed with getting the price of my next fix. I started back on heroin, but it was not always available, so I ended up shooting, snorting, popping, smoking, doing anything I could get. If I thought my life up till then had been bad, I was now introduced to an indescribable new nightmare. I had laughed at people who believed in Heaven or Hell, but I became more and more certain that Hell did exist.

I moved into an old abandoned house on skid row in Vancouver. There was only the shell of the house left as there had been a major fire and most of the walls and roof had caved in. The police would not enter for fear of falling through the floor, or having a wall fall in on them. Also there were the rats, mice, and cockroaches. Only the most desperate or lunatic fringe people would enter.

We slept on a filthy old mattress that was covered with stains, lice, and bedbugs, not to mention fleas and crabs. The mattress would hold about five bodies and there would often be fights for a spot. Our blankets were old newspapers covered with puke. This was the place we called home. The only other item we had was an old pot in which we could boil or heat water on a fire in the backyard; one tea bag could survive the second round if not given too much of a pounding. I had a very distorted view of reality but I could relate to the tea bag, as it got weaker and weaker—that was the story of my life.

I had been self-destructive from a very early age, full of fear and frustration. I tried to find a place where I could feel better, then I was told to take a drink and I would feel better. I did, and I felt ten feet tall. Then it was suggested to smoke a joint and I would feel better yet, then pep pills, bennys, Nembutals, Percodan—all the time just trying to feel better. Just like the tea bag, my hope, faith, strength and life was being drained out of me, and I could only wish that my life would end soon. I had become a zombie. My mind was going fast.

It was not long before I realized that my will to survive was diminishing. I thoroughly hated myself, was sure that no one else could understand me, and did not realize how sick I was. I felt overwhelmingly guilty because I was not able to look after my wife and kids. Because living had become worse than dying I started planning suicide. I was sure I had no friends left and I did not want to place the burden of my burial on my wife, so I made elaborate plans to dispose of my body when I killed myself.

After five or six drinks I would black out and

not remember anything until I woke up. I was a lousy driver when I drank—every time I tried to drive after drinking, I had an accident—so I planned to rent a car, drive to the Rocky Mountains, get drunk and drive off a cliff. Because the roads in the mountains were so treacherous, drivers were warned not to drive on them in bad weather, especially if they had been drinking. As I recall, the road was a two-lane highway with many curves and cliffs that dropped hundreds of feet. Looking down from your car you could see the tops of trees. In the best of weather and conditions you had to be extremely careful. Many stories were told of people disappearing over the side and never being heard from again. It seemed like the perfect way out.

During one of my attempts at sobriety while working as a telemarketing salesman, I had accumulated enough money to get the car. I drove to Penticton, B.C., which is approximately one hundred fifty miles into the mountains. I left Vancouver on a Friday night and I was determined that it would be my last trip. There was a neighbour who had been friendly to me, and I remember knocking on his door, giving him my key and telling him that if I did not come back he could have my radio and anything else he wanted from my apartment.

When I arrived in Penticton that Friday night, I checked into the Penticton Hotel and proceeded with my plan by getting drunk. Saturday morning I awoke sick as a dog, as usual. The first thing I did was get on my knees in the washroom—my habit was to kneel alongside the toilet and try to throw up the poison that I drank the night before—I can assure you it was not to pray. It did occur to me to say a prayer while I was on my knees, but I thought of my father's hypocrisy, and also of the shame that I had brought on my family and friends. My one and only prayer at this time was, "God help me!" even though I was sure he wasn't listening.

When the shakes subsided a little I got dressed and went looking for a drink. I had a feeling of relief because I was sure this was my last "morning after." All I can remember about that day is that I cried a lot. It rained all day and, because alcohol is a depressant, with each drink I felt worse. I bought a twenty-six ounce bottle of Canadian Club Whiskey, placed it on the front seat of the car, then continued to get drunk. I was certain that there wasn't a single human being in this world who would miss me. In fact, I was sure that many would be glad to see me go. I didn't blame them.

The time arrived for me to leave. There had been a steady downpour of rain all day. It was, or seemed to be, dark. I cannot remember much about leaving town and heading into the Rockies. In fact, the last thing that I remember is leaving Penticton, then my mind went blank. My next conscious moment was when I opened my eyes, looked at the ceiling and tried to figure out where I was. After a few moments I realized that I was back in my apartment in Vancouver. To put it mildly, I was shocked. There seemed no possible way that I could have driven that car all the way home! My only recollection of the trip home was car headlights shining in my eyes. From past experiences, knowing my capacity for alcohol, the only way to describe my condition was dead-drunk—I know that I had consumed enough alcohol to pass out several times.

The first thing I did when I rolled out of bed was go to the front window to check the car. The right front wheel was parked on the sidewalk but there was no damage that I could see. As I recall, it was about six A.M. and it took me a good half-hour to get down and back the car off the sidewalk. The front seat was all wet—my trademark, and something that happened quite often after I passed out. The whiskey bottle was still on the front seat, but there was only about four ounces left in it. I had drunk twenty-two ounces on the trip.

There had been many occasions in my past when I had taken chances with my life—I had been shot; I had been in wild car chases; knives had been thrown at me. I had fought with a knife and still had the scars to remind me. But this was altogether different. The more I thought about it, the more amazed I became at being alive.

I had to talk to someone about it, so I called my A.A. sponsor. All he could suggest was that I probably picked up a hitchhiker, who then drove the car. I asked him why a hitchhiker would park the car with the right front wheel on the sidewalk. Also, it wasn't likely that the hitchhiker would have sat on the seat that I had pissed on.

I have given up trying to find an explanation for what happened, and I don't care anymore. It was just another of the many strange things that happened to me. I was convinced that I could not do anything right. I knew that I could not live right. I couldn't even die right.

CHAPTER NINE

PRESSURE

I vaguely recall someone sitting on a bed talking to me. He looked familiar. I kept seeing his face and hearing him talking to me. I later learned that I was in a flophouse run by the city of Vancouver and that the person talking to me was Don, my sponsor from A.A. He had found me incoherent on the street and brought me here. He came to visit every day and nursed me back to health and sanity. After a couple of months of regular sleep and meals, and attending a clinic for daily Methadone shots, I began to act like a human being again, but a very depressed one. I believe now that it's a good thing I didn't know how far I had to go to recover or I would have seen it as hopeless and I would never have tried.

My A.A. sponsor, Don M., suggested that I enter a treatment centre for alcoholics. I had been in many of them before and they had not helped me, but what did I have to lose? I asked him to put my name on the list. He called back; they would have room for me on Friday, and he would give me a lift out there.

The Maple Ridge Treatment Centre was located in the beautiful little town of Maple Ridge, B.C., about forty miles from Vancouver. It had a good reputation. I knew many ex-patients who recommended it highly. They also informed me that success depended on the patient; the staff could help me only if I wanted to help myself. This sounded good to me, so I determined to work hard to get sober and stay sober. I was willing to do anything they wanted.

The first thing they did was give me a complete medical. I was surprised at the results. The doctor found that I had a busted eardrum, and that I had had it for quite a while. There was no use doing anything about it then, he said, adding that my Adam's apple was not where it was supposed to be; it was left of centre. No wonder my tie was always crooked!

After the medical they gave me a counsellor, Frank Riddle, who was to take me under his wing and try to get me through the hard spots. Frank was a terrific guy, but I am sure he deserved better. He got more and more frustrated as the days went by, and he always had that far-away look in his eye. I confided in him and was as honest as I knew how to be. He got me interested in the Twelve Steps and told me that if I would take them seriously I could become a happy man. He also told me that the steps had changed his life, and could change mine. I wanted to believe him because my life was a disaster. Anything would be better than what I was putting myself through. I know in my heart that I sincerely wanted to change. Frank told me that we would go through and complete the first five steps before I left the treatment centre. That would give me a good foundation. I could finish the steps with my sponsor when I hit the street.

The steps are really very simple, as long as you have something to work them with, such as a mind. But I had such severe mental disorders that it was hard to grasp even the simplest explanations. I had been conniving and scheming and conning for so long just to survive on the street that I didn't know how not to. I had learned to not trust anyone, especially someone you could not see, like God. However, I decided to give it my best shot. The first step was to admit that I was powerless over alcohol and that my life had become unmanageable. I certainly could admit this, but they told me that I had to fully accept it, which took me a long time.

The second step involved coming to believe that a power greater than myself could restore my sanity. The counsellors were very painstaking in explaining this step. They explained each word. We "came," then we "came to," and finally we "came to believe." I was conscientious in my efforts to understand the steps well and I felt that I really was accomplishing something.

The third step required me to make a decision to turn my will and my life over to the care of God as I understood Him. I did not want to do this step because I had my doubts about whether He would accept me. I was told to just make the decision.

For the fourth step I had to make a searching and fearless moral inventory of myself. This took me over a week. You are supposed to write down everything; all the defects you can find. I was as honest as I could be and tried to put on paper every rotten thing about myself. It wasn't pleasant, but I tried to do it to the best of my ability. I was surprised to find I had some positive traits. I loved animals, and was always bringing stray cats home, and I was always a sucker for a hard-luck story; in fact, I often went out of my way to help someone worse off than myself. Perhaps I had compassion, or even kind-heartedness. Or maybe I could relate to a person's suffering. What a relief it was to find out that I was not completely rotten. I found the truth in the old saying: "There is some good in the worst of us, and some bad in the best of us."

After step four I was drained and wanted to complete step five as soon as I could. It was to admit to God, to myself, and to another human being the exact nature of my wrongs. This was a humbling experience. I went to see the minister who came around once a week to do my fifth step, to "unload all the garbage," as they say. He tried to make it easy for me, and I appreciated that. After telling him about all my liabilities I felt so guilty that there was no way that I could mention that I might have a couple of assets.

My time in the treatment centre was coming to an end—I had been in the facility for almost three months and was anxiously waiting to hit the street and start my new life. My counsellor kept telling me about all the new benefits I would receive as a result of practicing the steps and I believed him. He stressed the importance of getting a job, being honest and not conning anymore. He told me to go to meetings every day, to pray, and to get busy filling out job applications. Because I was sincere about changing, I did everything I was told and more.

The fellow who ran the treatment centre had a contract with the city to pick up garbage and, because I really wanted to become responsible I worked as a garbage man during the last month of my treatment. I was so proud of my blisters that I showed them off to everyone. They were the first blisters I ever earned, and although the money I earned was pretty important, the ego-deflation, self-discipline and hard work were greater benefits. Every time we emptied a load of garbage at the dump, I pictured some of my personal garbage going with it. Oh, how I wanted to change and be the person that my dear Mom wanted me to be.

My sponsor in Vancouver said I could stay at his place until I found a place of my own. I was feeling great and was full of new hope and determined that this time nothing would stop me from reaching my goal of contented sobriety. Each night I attended an A.A. meeting, as the counsellor suggested. At the fourth or fifth meeting I noticed a really attractive woman sitting in the centre of the room so I went over and introduced myself.

Marie and I hit it off right away. After the meeting we went to a restaurant for coffee and she told me that her husband had passed away and that she had just sold their big house and moved into a new apartment. I moved in to her apartment and picked up some pot to make things more exciting. I could admit being addicted to alcohol, but I had been using different types of drugs for years and not admitting that I was addicted. That first night, after a couple of joints, we began getting to know each other. She had really accomplished a lot. She had been a high school teacher, and was now working on the administrative staff of a large and popular bank. She also had an Alfa Romeo car plus everything money could buy.

I was at the other end of the totem pole and had nothing. I was very much impressed with her lifestyle and experiences. She then asked me what my line was. When I'm high on pot, anything is likely to come out of my mouth. So I jokingly told her I was a muff diver! Not having any idea what that was, she asked me the kind of work a muff diver did. I tried to make it as impressive as possible by telling her we were taken out to sea in ships in the early hours of the morning. We had to prepare our diving gear and make sure we had plenty of oxygen, and we had to prepare the stun guns for the sharks and piranhas that were likely to attack us. We even had a special spray for killer whales. She became so excited that she began calling me her hero. I had really impressed her. I had no idea where this lie would lead me.

A few days later, I drove out to the treatment centre to see my counsellor, Frank Riddle, and tell him all the good news. I was so proud of myself and wanted to let everyone know that the treatment really worked. Frank was very happy to see me, but when I invited him out to see my new car, his face changed and he asked me where I had got it. When I told him that Marie had bought it for me, he gave me a sad look and said "Mike, you're conning again." I immediately thought that Frank was jealous because his car was about ten years old and mine was brand new. Anyway, I was sure the patients were impressed with my new benefits.

The following week I paid my last visit to the treatment centre, just before Marie and I went on a vacation to Hawaii. As I was leaving and old Frank was waving good-bye, I could not understand why he was not happy for me. If only I could have understood. Lying on the beach on the island of Maui, Hawaii, I looked up at the sky and thought, "Why didn't I start practicing the steps sooner?" I was sure that these benefits were a direct result of the steps, and, who knows, maybe they were. Mom always said that God works in mysterious ways. I know for sure that my level of contentment and happiness had gone way up!

Marie insisted that I open a bank account with a healthy deposit she provided, as it would give me more confidence. She was right. It gave me so much confidence that it caused me to become a confidence-man again. The scheming, lying and conniving returned as bad as ever. I don't think it had ever really left me. Since I had confessed to Marie all the rotten things I had done in the past, and how much I wanted to be honest, she could not say that I didn't warn her. My only job now was driving her to work in the morning and picking her up after work. I guess I was playing the only game I knew, and although I had a deep desire for change, change can be a slow and difficult process.

Marie was doing very well at work and the bank was holding an Awards Night for the executive staff. Many top executives from the main offices in Ottawa and Montreal would be in attendance. She had a ticket for me, as each participant for an award could bring a husband, wife, or friend. When we walked in the hotel, we were greeted by her many friends and associates and took our places at a long table. Marie introduced me to so many people. I felt really important.

There was a lull between the awards and speakers and everyone was nice and quiet at our table. All of a sudden, some loud mouth hollered down the table "By the way, Marie, what line is Mike in?" Marie being so proud of me could not help but holler back that I was a muff diver! There seemed to be a stunned moment of silence, then screams of laughter. To make it worse, I later won a door prize, which was a bottle of champagne. Knowing that the story had now spread, I had to endure the snickering and finger pointing as I made my way up to the podium to accept the prize.

When Marie found out what a muff diver really was, she was so aghast she refused to go back to work. She quit her job and said it was the best thing that happened to her. She actually thought it was very funny.

We left for Montreal shortly thereafter. In my sick mind I thought that it would be a triumphant return and my wife and kids would be proud of me. I had achieved a great success out west and now deserved their love and respect. But kids are not as dumb as that; they could see that I had not changed, and that I was still the phoney I had always been.

It was not long before Marie and I were drinking again. She had to do everything because I was completely useless when I drank. Finally, we decided to go to the Maple Leaf Farm Treatment

Center in Vermont, which had a good reputation. Many an alcoholic that had gone there had not drunk again. I had been there for treatment a few times in the past, but it hadn't worked for me. I determined that this time was going to be different. And it was: We stayed there twenty-eight days and, since March 30, 1975, I have not taken a drink or a drug. But I was not out of the woods yet.

Marie went back to work at the bank in Montreal and I had a lot of time on my hands, so I started looking in the newspapers for something to do. I came across an ad for video games. It said that people could double their money in six months if they bought a game and found a good location for it. There were some of these games already on locations downtown, where you could not help but notice that they were very popular with young people, and were taking in a lot of money. I bought one and located it downtown at the YMCA. One of the nearby universities was overcrowded, and many students were transferred to the YMCA to attend classes. At my suggestion, my game was placed in the cafeteria and started paying off immediately. This first game took in over two hundred dollars a week, which I split with the manager of the YMCA, and everyone was happy.

I started working for a games company and found out that what they were paying for the games was half as much as I paid for mine. I also found that nobody was distributing the games on the East Coast, and that the company was not taking advantage of every opportunity for making money. For instance, they bought the games and sold them from their own showroom, which was next to their offices. I suggested that they put the games on location as soon as they arrived, to make money and get the best locations before someone else grabbed them. I also suggested selling the games from the locations, but they didn't take up that suggestion.

It was not long before I convinced Marie that there was a lot of money to be made, so she quit her job and we packed our belongings, sold our furniture and headed for the East Coast. We arrived in Halifax full of ambition and optimism. We rented offices on Barrington Street and set up a company called Maritime Distributors. We ordered the first ten games the day we arrived, and were very excited when they arrived. We found great locations and took in more money than we had expected. We placed a couple in Dalhousie University and each one brought in over three hundred dollars a week.

Marie and I placed ads in the paper telling people how to double their money in a year, or how to get rich with a small investment. I also called the local newspaper and told them about the new billion-dollar video game industry. They sent a couple of reporters down to our office to see us demonstrate the new games and they gave us a big write-up. This free advertising gave us the push we needed to succeed. We began getting orders for five and ten games at a time, and we were selling them for $2,995 each. We only paid $1,000 each for the games, and when someone ordered ten we discounted them to $2,500 per game. We didn't even have to unpack them. At $1,500 per game, there was a terrific profit in merely running down to the airport, changing the bill of lading on the boxes, and forwarding them to their new destinations.

We noticed that as soon as someone bought one game and began realizing a good profit, he would be back to buy more. We suggested that the best locations were going fast, and that now was the time to buy. I charged one hundred dollars for a location; two hundred dollars for insurance in case a game broke down and we sent a repair man free of charge. This was the best scam that I had ever come up with, and they called it a "business."

My bank manager was taking me out for lunch, my lawyer was always dropping in, and both were letting me know that they would be glad to invest in my business.

We spent Sundays rolling the quarters that the collectors picked up from the games. There were some games and locations that were not for sale. By then we had three games at Dalhousie University and they were too profitable to sell; we took customers there and showed them the money they were taking in. We had a salesman who would go out and find the best locations for the games in Halifax, or Dartmouth, which is right across the bridge, and in other nearby towns and cities. The games and locations that were for sale often returned our initial outlay—$1,000 in quarters—before we sold them; in some cases they produced two or three times that before we sold them.

Business got better; in fact, I opened up another company, Marelco Manufacturing, to build the games so that I could avoid paying the import duties. Also, this way I produced the games at half the cost. I also got interested in giant television screens and projection systems. There were a couple of these in the larger drinking establishments where I had located my games. I heard that they had cost the proprietors over $4,000 each.

I checked them out at a convention in Chicago and found that I could get all the parts from Wisconsin for the projection system; get the Kodak screens from Rochester, New York; buy the fourteen-inch Quasar TV sets in Canada; and assemble them into a system for less than $1,500. My plan was to put these into locations free of charge, as long as they allowed us to operate our games and take one hundred percent of the profit. We were also getting into the pinball business, because we took them as trade-ins, or as credit on new video games. We were in the big time.

When I had completed my treatment at Maple Leaf Farm, they had warned me that I would have to go to lots of A.A. meetings. I knew this was good advice and I tried to attend as many meetings as I could, but as business got better I went on an ego trip and became so self-centred that I became heavily sedated with my own self-importance. A.A. was not an important part of my plans any-more. I gradually cut my meetings from four or five a week to one. By then my mind had become so wrapped up in wheeling and dealing that I did not hear a word that was said at the meetings any-way. I had what is commonly called in the A.A. program "self-will run riot."

The third step of the A.A. program was to

make a decision to turn our will and our lives over to the care of God—as we understand Him. At the Maple Leaf Farm in Vermont they had suggested that I accept God as a higher power, but because of the way my Mother died it was very hard to find a concept of God that I could live with. And, now that I was so important, turning my life over to Him was out of the question.

I was flying to New York, Chicago, Montreal, and many other places on "business," or so I thought. But the real reason was to find new women to satisfy my sex drive. As I became more irritable, my trips increased and I conned myself into believing that this was good therapy because my nerves were bad. But I now realize that, as an alcoholic, my disease and my alcoholic mentality allowed me to replace alcohol with an obsession for sex, gambling, larceny. I was an addictive person, and it seemed easier to fall into a bad habit than a good one.

Success can be disastrous for any alcoholic, and it was especially so for me. It is one thing to achieve success, which I had done many times, but it is more important to know how to *handle* success. I did not have the right stuff. I was unstable, irresponsible, full of fear, and as my obligations and responsibilities added up, I became panic-stricken. My fears mounted until my nerves were completely shot and I thought I was on the verge of a nervous breakdown. I even had difficulty walking across a busy street. Oh, how I wanted to escape! Then my fear-stricken mind came up with a great idea. We would open new offices in Montreal and I would go there to escape and let Marie handle Halifax, because I thought she was much better at the business.

What I did not know at the time was that due to lack of A.A. meetings and the help of my sponsor, I had become a dry drunk. This was worse than a drinking alcoholic or a wet drunk. It says in the Big Book of Alcoholics Anonymous that we get a daily reprieve contingent on the maintenance of our spiritual condition, but I still could not even accept the fact that A.A. was a spiritual program. Eventually, I went back to the treatment centre in Vermont and Marie came to help me any way she could. This time I left the treatment centre after two weeks because Marie had to get back to Halifax and I had to manage the Montreal office.

My emotional and mental disorders were becoming worse. I would have the most terrible nightmares and wake up screaming and shaking with the DTs (delirium tremens). I'd hallucinate that snakes and rats were crawling up and down the walls. I would be in a state of intense fear or terror. I felt that people were going to smash through the windows or doors, to tear me apart and murder me at any moment. These nightmares were so realistic that I woke up soaking wet with perspiration, shaking so much that I could not go back to sleep until daylight. Only another alcoholic, or someone experiencing withdrawal from drugs, can relate to these feelings. I was becoming paranoid and displaying hallucinations and marked behavioural deterioration. Looking back, it is hard to believe that I came through these experiences without going completely mad.

I had read many times that most businesses fail because of bad management—ours was no exception. The great business deals that I thought would provide so many solutions only brought more pressure and responsibilities, until there seemed to be no way out but to close down the business and escape. The people working for me were mystified at the decisions I was making, and thought I had lost my head but there was no way that I could explain my actions. I was like a drowning man, and the only way I could survive was to get rid of all the extra weight. Marie could not handle the new responsibilities she had, and she started drinking. We were a couple of sick and desperate alcoholics who were on the verge of alcoholic convulsions. Eventually we had to get rid of the stock in Halifax. And what a relief that was.

We had rented a lovely home and bought beautiful new furniture. We had been so very happy and confident when we moved in that we thought our troubles were all behind us. We lost it all. Now I was full of remorse because, as usual, I had failed again.

CHAPTER TEN

MY MIRACLE

These experiences were taking their toll on my health. I was losing weight and had many coughing fits. My skin was turning yellow and occasionally I would spit blood. Marie kept suggesting that I go and see a doctor, but I kept putting it off until the coughing got so bad that I had to stop going to A.A. meetings. Every time I went it seemed that my coughing got worse; people turned around to look at me, making me want to crawl through the floor. I had always been sensitive about my coughing. At a very early age I had acquired a bronchial condition, probably from sleeping outside as a kid, and whenever I coughed a lot I would think it was my bronchitis acting up. At A.A. meetings there was so much smoke that even if you were healthy it made you cough.

There were other things to worry about. The whites of my eyes were not white any longer; they had turned yellow. I continued to lose weight, so I finally followed Marie's suggestion and went to see a doctor. This doctor was a man I had always admired and respected. He also was a member of A.A. and had helped many thousands of members in the past, including Marie and myself. After he gave me a physical examination and heard the way I was coughing, he referred me to a Dr. Edinger, who had offices downtown at the Seaforth Medical Building. He got me an appointment for the following day, a Thursday.

After examining me, Dr. Edinger sent me for x-rays at a clinic in the same building. He told me that I could go home after the x-rays, and that he would call me with the results the following day. You can imagine my surprise when he called me and told me that I had lung cancer, and that he had notified the Montreal General Hospital for a bed. I had to stay close to the phone, because as soon as a bed was available I would be notified.

My first impulse was to get drunk, and I continued to think that until the phone rang on Monday morning—the hospital had a bed for me. It still surprises me when I remember that I got to the hospital without taking a drink. My pattern for many years when I received bad news or had a lot of pain was to escape into the bottle. This time Marie seemed to be in more pain than I was. Every time she looked at me she started crying and even though I told her it made me feel worse, she couldn't stop.

I had read a story in Reader's Digest about a fellow who had the same type of operation that I was getting. He said that if he had it to do over again he would refuse to have it, and he ended up dying six months later anyway. My doctors, however, assured me that my chances of recovery were good with the operation. At the time my mind was so messed up that I could not think straight.

My relationship with God had been terrible since my Mother died; it had never been very good anyway, but for a while I would get up and walk out of A.A. meetings when there was too much God-talk. I had thought of myself as an atheist, but like that old story about the troops in the trenches, when the bullets start flying past your head you can become a believer awful fast. Such as five minutes after I got the phone call about my lung cancer.

I brought a lot of books to the hospital, planning on getting spiritual very fast. My Mom's words—that there is more wrought by prayer than this world dreams of—kept coming back, along with the way she impressed me that day we went to the courthouse, as if she had received a message directly from God. I did not know how to pray very well, so I asked Mom to "pray for me, wherever you are." I knew that if there was a God, Mom would be close by. I asked for another chance at changing, at becoming a decent human being, and at trying to follow in my Mom's footsteps. It was hard to believe that this was the same guy who had been trying to kill himself just a couple of years before. It didn't seem like much had changed in the meantime, but somehow I got the will to live.

Monday and Tuesday were uneventful, except that I received fruit baskets and a lot of plants and bouquets of flowers. I remember thinking that the flowers were a bad omen, and that the people who sent them knew somehow that my number was up. I had been told not to smoke, but with the stress, there was no way I could stop. I did cut down quite a bit.

Then it was Wednesday and four or five doctors were at the foot of my bed. I asked one of them if there could possibly have been a mistake and that it was not really lung cancer. I remember so well his answer to me: "Sorry," he answered "but pictures don't lie." They informed me that the operation would take place the following morning. My hopes were dwindling fast. That afternoon the intern came in to shave my chest, and after he left I had my third cigarette that day. I was quite proud of myself, because by that time of day I would ordinarily have smoked a full pack.

I was sitting at the foot of my bed, just day-dreaming, when in walked a doctor whom I recognized as Doctor David Mulder, the surgeon who was to perform the operation the following morning. I wish that I could remember his exact words, but they were something like, "Mike, pre-pare yourself for a shock." I responded, "What the hell would shock me now? I've been in shock ever since I got the news of my x-rays."

But his next words really did shock me. He said he was looking at the x-ray of my lungs, going over the section that he was going to remove, when, for some strange reason, he looked down at the name and birth date on the chart. He calculated my age and found that I was only twenty-nine, and he figured that there must be a mistake since he knew I was really forty-five. The height on the chart was five foot seven but I was five foot ten and one-half. There were enough mistakes for him to make a phone call to a Dr. Rabinovitch who was in charge of the x-ray clinic.

It was hard to believe, but he found another x-ray for a Michael Maloney who had passed through the clinic two days before me. They confirmed that the x-rays had been mixed up and my doctor was given the wrong x-ray. I was stunned to say the least, and asked him what I should do now. He said I could get up and go home. My next action was to look skyward and thank God for a miracle. I had difficulty praying but I did ask for help, promising to do the very best I could to help others and to prove my gratitude by trying to be the best I could be. If you had seen the condition I was in on entering the hospital, you would also believe in miracles.

After leaving the hospital, I felt so sorry for the Michael Maloney who was to take my place that I tried to get in touch with him. The first place I looked was the Montreal phone book but there were no Michael Maloneys listed there, but there was one Michel (Michael in French) and I called him, but he did not know what I was talking about. Then I tried to get some information about him from the hospital, but I ran into a dead end. I finally decided to leave well enough alone, but the more I considered the odds against this happening, or this just being an accident, the more I believed in miracles. First, there must be at least fifty x-ray clinics in Montreal. This man must have gone to the same one that I went to, and he would have to have had the same symptoms.

There were so many unanswered questions, and it just got more and more frustrating as I searched for the answers. Soon I came to realize that I did not need the answers. All I really needed was a little more faith in God. I knew that my Mom was still looking after me, and that her prayers were probably responsible for my miracle. I thanked God and promised to really try to change my life, and I also prayed for a grateful heart.

It took a while to get my health back. My natural colour returned, my weight gradually increased to where it had been before, my coughing became normal again, and I had not spit blood since I left the hospital. Since I had been given a full physical recovery I was determined to work hard for a mental and spiritual recovery.

There was a new term in my vocabulary: self-conquest. Although it was not in Webster's Dictionary, it was always on my mind and it became more and more important to me. Ever since I had been a kid and had heard the old man tell me that I was no good, never had been any good, and never would be any good, that concept was ingrained in me. Over the years I also heard remarks like, "he'll never change," and "a leopard never changes its spots." Well, now I felt that it was important that I try to change.

Alcoholism is a three-fold disease: physical, mental and spiritual. After my physical recovery, I knew there had to be a purpose for my being alive. My next challenge was to recognize my mental disorders and try to find solutions to them. One of the most serious problems I had was recognizing and accepting that I was very sick mentally. I thought that virtue and principles were weaknesses that you found in suckers and straight people, people who didn't know any better. I thought I was pretty smart because I was good at scheming, conning, and hustling a buck. A sponsor once told me that I had the price of everything and the value of nothing. I had street smarts.

Marie and I decided to go out West again thinking our chances for recovery would be better there. Although we didn't recognize it, what we were really doing was going on another geographical cure, trying to escape reality. We sold the rest of what business we had left in Montreal and headed for Calgary, which, along with the province of Alberta, was thriving because of the new oil discoveries.

We checked into a motel and started looking for an apartment. The rents were very high because of all the new people arriving each day. I came across a help-wanted ad for a janitor, which would provide a free apartment, plus a small wage. This was a good break and we took advantage of it. My next lucky break was in hearing about an A.A. convention taking place in Penticton, B.C.

The theme of the convention was "An Attitude of Gratitude," and the speaker was a real miracle. He had been involved with the Mafia in New York, until his disease progressed to the point where he became useless to himself and everyone else. People had tried to steer him to the Alcoholics Anonymous program, and he had even attended a few meetings, but he kept returning to his first love alcohol until he finally found himself on the Bowery. He was literally dying from the effects of alcohol. He was throwing up blood and was so sick that he was incapable of doing anything for himself.

A passerby, noticing how desperately sick he was, lying there in the street, asked if there was anything he could do for him. Jack, the alcoholic, was surprised to hear himself ask the stranger to please call A.A. Shortly after that, a little Jewish fellow and his wife arrived and took Jack and he was admitted to Bellevue Hospital, where he commenced his long road to recovery.

He told a wonderful, inspirational story that I will always remember. Jack spoke about the Twelve Steps in his message, and after the meeting I approached him. I told him the trouble I was having with the steps, how frustrated and angry I got when I tried to follow them and failed, and that I knew I was doing them all wrong. He had a simple solution to my problem. "Mike," he said, "you can't do the steps wrong. You can only do them to the best of your ability. You don't need a college education to practice the steps. God knows that you are trying to do what is right and that is all that really matters."

It was such a simple answer, and afterwards whenever I got hung up on the steps, I would remember what good old Jack had told me. At that convention I also came to realize how important an attitude of gratitude was for anything in my life. I was so resentful that I could not drink like other people that I became more and more miserable, and soon my personality got so bad that I was impossible to live with.

Today I place great value on gratitude, and realize how important it is to me. I pray to God for a grateful heart. I have told many of my sponsees (those whom I sponsor) that there are three ingredients necessary for contented sobriety, the three *G*s: God, guts, and gratitude. For twenty years I had been trying to do it my way and was getting nowhere. Now, as I practiced the steps, asking God for help, things got better.

An opportunity came for me to work at a recovery centre in Calgary. Gordie, the manager, was a terrific guy to whom I had gone for help many times. He was a great example for me. He had been a patient in a mental hospital for many years before attending A.A. meetings and the last time he was released he started going to night school to further his education. He also became a regular visitor of the bullpen at police headquarters, looking for drunks he could help. This is called Twelve Step Work, and is so very important for an A.A. member. Old-timers in A.A. say that "if you want to keep this program, you have to give it away or share it," and Gordie always did that. Luckily I was one of the recipients!

I loved the job at the recovery centre, and although I did not know much about counselling at the time, I tried to impress on the patients how important the A.A. program was in my recovery. I told them that if they wanted to get well, all they

had to do was to attend A.A. meetings and practice the Twelve Steps.

My hunger for knowledge was great as I began
to realize how little I knew. If I wanted to help
people, I had to know what I was talking about.
Gordie was a great example to me. He had worked
each day, gone to school at night, and finally
entered university where he earned a degree in
psychology. This impressed me, and I was always
asking his advice and picking his brains. I admired
and respected him so much. I will always love the
man for all he did for me. He left a lasting impression, and I hope that someday I may be able to
follow in his footsteps. He is, in my estimation, a
great success because he achieved what he went
after, and did not let ego or money problems deter
him from his main goal, which was carrying the
message to the alcoholic who still suffers. He is
still carrying the message.

On the wall in Gordie's office, for all to see,
was the Eleventh Step: "Sought through prayer
and meditation to improve our conscious contact
with God, as we understood Him, praying only for
knowledge of His will for us and the power to
carry that out." Gordie lived by this step, and also
the Twelfth Step: "Having had a spiritual awakening as the result of these steps, we tried to carry

this message to alcoholics and to practice these principles in all our affairs."

One of the most foolish things I did while working at the centre was to lose my temper with a patient; it taught me a lesson I hope I'll always remember. I got into an argument for some unknown reason, and one word led to another until the patient told me to fuck off. He bruised my ego, to say the least. At that particular time, as I see it now, I was an imbecile running around trying to impress people with how important I was.

Gordie heard about the argument and he called me into his office to ask what had happened. Of course I told him that it was the patient's fault, and tried to justify my actions, but he was wise to my bullshit. He quietly explained that the patient had every right to be sick. The patient, he explained, was trying to recover from a serious disease, but the staff was there to be understanding, patient, and tolerant. We should not react to outbursts by the patients. That experience was a valuable lesson that I still profit from. It is so important that I try to think wisely before reacting.

It became quite obvious to me that I acted more like a patient than a staff member. I also began to recognize some of my shortcomings. On the one hand, I had a criminal personality; on the other hand, I had an alcoholic mentality. In other words, I was really messed up and I knew that trying to unravel my problems and finding solutions to them would take a lot of hard work. One thing that really bothered me was my lack of schooling. I had never stayed still long enough to get promoted to a higher grade. If I remember correctly, I never got higher than the fourth grade. Deciding to go back to school, I filled out an application and the Alberta Vocational Centre accepted me into their academic upgrading program. So, at age fifty, I returned to school and I loved every minute of it.

I began reading everything I could put my hands on that might give me some answers to my many problems. Not only did I have to learn new habits and ideas, but I also had to unlearn bad habits. My thoughts became very important to me, so I tried to discipline my thinking.

In my class at school there were a lot of teenagers and people in their early twenties, and I remember being especially afraid of being laughed at. My girlfriend, Marie, had been a teacher at one time so I received a lot of help from her. Also, I devoured my schoolbooks and paid special attention to my homework so that I did not make mistakes. There were over twenty young people in my class and I found it so very important to be a good example. As a kid in school, and as a husband and father, I had been a bad example. Now was my chance to start turning things around.

Right from the start my efforts paid off, with my marks consistently in the high 90s, even the odd 100. Good marks made me work all the harder. The teacher was a great guy who complimented me often, and in whom I confided about my past. He encouraged me and helped me so much. When kids started coming over to my desk to check their answers or ask questions, I was a little embarrassed, but the teacher seemed to encourage them to come to me. He would correct my papers first, then I would compare my answers with theirs and correct their papers. I was so proud of myself.

The benefits I received from school were not recognizable until much later, when I took a new inventory of myself. In the past it had been very discouraging to take a personal inventory because I had so many liabilities and so very few assets. Now, I was beginning to develop some self-esteem, and self-respect; I was convinced that my efforts at becoming a decent human being were starting to pay off. My efforts at carrying the message to other alcoholics, my Twelve Step Work, were very gratifying, too. There is an old saying around A.A., it is hard to give away something that you haven't got. Well, I began to think I had something to give away, something that others didn't have, and the results were encouraging. My decision to leave the Renfrew Recovery Centre to attend school was a good one then. After just a few months, I had to make another big decision.

This one was really hard. I had come so far in just a few months and I had come to really love this school. I had also started an A.A. meeting for any students who had a drinking or drug problem. John was a new member of A.A., and I agreed to become his sponsor. I met John while he was at the recovery centre. He had started a cement and asphalt paving business and I had lent him some money to get started. The business really took off. It was a gold mine. He asked me a few times to come and work for him. I refused, but then he came back with an offer of $3,000 a month, just to supervise the jobs and give estimates on new jobs for cement or asphalt paving work. John was doing so well that he had just rented larger offices in a shopping centre. He had also just bought his own cement-mixer truck.

I had been afraid for him, because I knew from past experiences of the danger of success for the alcoholic. To be able to handle success, we need to be responsible, stable, tolerant, patient, but an alcoholic's frustration level is very low. We can barely handle the job of everyday living—just meeting the daily challenges without a drink is an accomplishment. Most of us are so full of fear that when we take on more responsibilities this creates more fear, and we usually short-circuit.

But having warned John of all the pitfalls he could face, I decided to join him because I really thought that by taking some of the load off his back it would relieve the pressure enough that he would be able to handle it. I soon realized that I was on an ego trip and that if one alcoholic is bad for business, two alcoholics are twice as bad. The road to hell, as they say, is paved with good intentions.

It was not long after I took this job that my interests changed. I was back in familiar surroundings doing the things that I knew best—wheeling and dealing, working all the angles, conning, and playing the big shot. I lost all or most of my interest in the Twelve Steps and also cut down on going to meetings. I had taken a wrong turn in the road and was headed right back to where I had started. I knew that whatever progress I had made towards living a good, decent life was going by the board—I was in a state of regression. It was not long before the fears of old, the guilt, the resentments, the hate, and most of all, the paranoia returned. I now justified my actions by conning myself that there was a good reason for doing the things I did.

When I thought I had lung cancer in the hospital, my prayer was that if God would give me another chance I would show my appreciation by changing my way of life and trying to help others who were as sick as I was. My guilt only increased with the memory of those prayers, but I was the type of character who, once started on the wrong road, could not seem to turn back. It seemed that I was so full of guilt and shame that I could not ask God or anyone else for help.

About that time, my health started to deteriorate again. John's business was going down the drain and things were so bad at home that Marie began to drink again and I started running around. Marie and I had been together for five years, but she could not seem to stay sober for any length of time. I broke up with Marie and she returned to the work at the bank.

My next job was with a frozen food company, Alberta's specialists in freezer meats and bulk food orders. They showed me a large poster of a dissected cow with the names of each section, then made me a food consultant. I became an instant expert with a fancy business card showing my qualifications. This was just another swindle. The company placed full-page ads in large-circulation newspapers, telling readers to simply fill out the coupon on the page and send it in. A food consultant would be sent out with information on how to save tons of money. My commission on the smallest order was at least a hundred bucks.

There was one girl, Margaret, who began to attend A.A. meetings and I had a crush on her. She became my assistant. She filled in the contracts. We were given an envelope full of leads, and we brought in as many as ten orders a day. We worked three or four days a week, and we made all the money we needed.

I was very attracted to Margaret so we rented a nice house, bought a new car, and furnished our house with new furniture. Everything was beautiful but, as usual, it was too good to last. My bad luck started when I found that after walking a block or two my legs started to ache. It soon got so bad that I went to see a doctor. He gave me some tests and said that I needed a bypass operation because of bad circulation. The following month I went into the hospital for the operation.

Margaret did not like hospitals, so she did not visit often. When she did come she socialized with the other patients and staff, practically ignoring me. I could not understand why she acted that way. One day, when my sponsor was leaving after one of his visits at the hospital. I asked him to go to my bank to cash a cheque for me. I was shocked an hour later when he phoned and said that the cheque had been refused as NSF. There had been over $7,000 in our account when I went into the hospital. It was a joint account that we could both cash cheques on—Margaret must have emptied the account. Then on the morning I was to go home I realized there was something really wrong. She did not show up to bring me home and I had to call my sponsor to get a lift. When I got home she wasn't there, and I became really worried.

My suspicions were justified—because of her addiction, Margaret was suffering from a chemical imbalance which caused her to act in a completely irresponsible and insane manner. On one occasion she woke up on an Indian reservation and could not remember how she got there. Another time she jumped off a bridge and did not know why. Under the influence she tried to self-destruct. She went completely insane; in fact, she had been locked up on a couple of occasions and the diagnosis was that she had a chemical imbalance. I could have told them that.

This was a very discouraging period of my

life. I reported our car stolen, although I knew Margaret had taken it, and the police picked it up. Margaret had tried to sell it. She ended up in the mental hospital called Ponoka and I had to give up the house, sell the furniture, and start back once again at square one.

When I went to see her, she did not recognize me. She had tried to run away from the hospital, so they increased her medication to such an extent that she was incoherent. She had become a zombie and did not know where she was. It was a long drive to Ponoka from Calgary, and it was very discouraging because we could not communicate—we sat in the canteen and stared at each other. I suggested to her doctor that she might be better off with less medication, but it was like talking to a wall.

There were a couple more visits with no improvement in her condition, but I asked that, if they saw any improvement, to let me know so I could come to see her. I have not seen her again.

My son Derek was now living in Calgary and I was staying at his place. I was really broken-hearted at what had happened to all of my beautiful dreams. It seemed that every time I came close to having a normal life, it eluded me and I had to start over again. I thought of suicide and made a decision to take all the painkillers I'd been given in one dose. That night, for some unknown reason, I got out of bed and knelt down and said a prayer. My thinking seemed to change and so I threw the pills down the toilet and thought "This is just another test and, with God's help, I can come through this crisis without any drugs or alcohol."

One day at a time things got better. I went to a retreat (an intensive weekend) at a Jesuit monastery, and came back with a more positive outlook. Things continued getting better. I met Bill, who was willing to bankroll me if I started another employment agency. He was managing a few buildings downtown and said he could let me have an office and the furniture I needed to start. Also he would provide me with the money to pay a secretary, and to pay for all the business cards, invoices, form letters. In other words, he would be my silent partner. In return, he expected fifty percent of the profits.

This went well for about five weeks but then he got cold feet. He had spent about $3,000, and he began coming in and complaining that he was short of money and that we would have to start paying our own bills. Unknown to him, I had put a business opportunity ad in the newspaper and had received a few bites.

One was from a young man who was very ambitious. He had a profitable restaurant downtown called Grandma Lee's and he was looking for another business deal, so I made him an offer that he liked. I told him about my ill health, and explained that because the business was increasing at such a fast pace I could not handle it alone. He took the bait, and when I suggested a price of $25,000 for forty-nine percent, he jumped at it. We agreed to see a lawyer the next day to draw up the papers for a partnership agreement.

My silent partner, Bill, did not know anything about this. He came in the following morning in a really bad mood and started raving about how much money this was costing him, that he was crazy to have become involved and that he might have to close the doors by the end of the week. We ended up having a big argument, and I finally asked him to give me forty-eight hours to come up with the money that he had invested, after which we would dissolve the partnership. My new partner, Danny, and I concluded our business with the lawyer and I deposited a certified cheque for $25,000 in my account.

The next day Bill came in with an itemized list that amounted to $3,700. 1 looked over his list and said that it looked all right to me and proceeded to write him a cheque for the full amount. He seemed to be shocked and mentioned that he thought I was broke. I told him my luck was getting better, and it certainly was.

The company was called Fast Action, the same name as the company I had started in Vancouver a few years before. We dealt in people, but this time it was not only hotel and restaurant people. We advertised that we could supply anyone with whatever tradesman they wanted: plumbers, electricians, carpenters—anyone. We were sending some people out to work, and we had thousands who came in to fill out applications. Our phones never stopped ringing and there was usually a line up in the hall of people trying to get in to fill out an application.

It sure looked like a thriving business and I guess it was, only I was not interested in running the business. I wanted to dress it up, make it look better, and sell fast, as soon as I got my hands on the money from Danny. I decided to go to Edmonton to open another agency, separate from the one in Calgary. This one had no problems. Everything went so smooth that I was even turning buyers away. As part of the dressing for the business, I had two real beautiful girls working for me—a blond and a brunette—as receptionist and secretary. I also rented lovely furniture and spread big potted plants around the office. My ads in the newspapers were now asking for oil workers and engineers. We needed everyone.

I think it was around this time that I began to realize that if there was an honest way to run a business and a crooked way, I seemed to prefer scheming, conniving, and conning. Ever since I had been a kid on the carnivals, and sold magazines, and later done fundraising, I had come to believe that what Barnum had said was true: "There is a sucker born every minute," and I wanted my share. I was an addictive person whose bad habits were hard to change. I was trying to practice the A.A. program, along with the Twelve Steps, so that I might become a decent human being. Although there was some improvement along the way, I was so well grounded in my bad habits, and I enjoyed them so much, they were hard to give up.

My thinking at the time was that if the other professions, such as doctors, lawyers, and engineers could practice their line of work in A.A., why the hell couldn't I? I considered myself a professional con artist, and, in my estimation, that was something to be proud of. Really, it was what I knew best, and when people would talk about honesty, my usual reaction was, "If I got honest I'd starve to death; and what lousy hypocrites." I finally began to realize that because I was dishonest I thought everyone else was, and also that because I was a liar I thought they were all liars, too. It was a strange way of thinking, but, as I said, I was very sick.

A young fellow called David came in about two weeks after I opened the office. He wanted to buy into my business, so I played games with him. He could see that more and more people were coming in every day, that the phones were always ringing, and that my secretary could often be heard yelling at the receptionist to find her twelve waiters and four busboys immediately.

David wanted to become a partner but I told him that it was hard to know the value of the business when it was improving at such a rapid rate. I told him to come and see me the next week because I was too busy to talk to him then. Knowing that other people were coming to see me as a result of my business opportunity ad made him more anxious to close a deal with me, so he would be in my way everywhere I went, wanting to talk business.

I finally told him that my price for forty-nine

percent of the business was $25,000, but that the money was not important. What I really wanted was a partner who was ambitious and who was not afraid to work twelve to fifteen hour days as the business increased. Also, I needed someone who could travel across the country as we opened more branches. "If I were not so busy, I would wait to take on a partner," I said, "but, as you can see, it is too much for one man. If you are serious, go out and get a certified cheque for $25,000. I'll draw up the papers and we'll go down the hall and see my lawyer." I had already spoken to the lawyer.

David left and he was back within the hour, all excited, with the cheque. We went to see the lawyer, who suggested that he draw up a legal partnership agreement. I said that we did not have the time or the money to get involved in legal manoeuvres. We both had agreed to keep our deal as simple as possible, and I also mentioned that my Mom's advice to me was that if I wanted to stay out of trouble I should stay away from doctors and lawyers.

Two weeks later I sold the other half of the business for the same price and left town. I explained that I had other business deals that had to be looked after, and that I just could not stay. When I left I assured them that I would be back, and that they could phone me at the Calgary office any time if they needed help. It was shortly after this that I sold out the rest of the Calgary branch, went on a nice holiday, and continued to open employment agencies across the country.

All this time I continued to go to A.A. meetings and associate with people in the program, because without the A.A. program I was sure that I would be back on drugs or alcohol. But there was something that was beginning to affect me, making me very uncomfortable. At the time I could not recognize what was bothering me, but later it became obvious that it was my conscience. It was becoming harder and harder to lie and con. My stories were not rolling off my tongue like they used to. Instead of getting better at my line of work, I was getting worse.

My thinking at the time was, "What the hell is the use of praying, things only get worse." But sometimes things have to get worse before they get better. What I now realize is that I was acquiring a new set of values, and that decency and principles, prayer and God were becoming more and more important to me. My new way of thinking could not live together with the old way. There were things that were happening to me that I considered bad luck at the time, but now believe to have been good luck.

After a vacation in Florida to visit my sister, I returned to Ottawa, Ontario, and opened another employment agency. I also started speaking at A.A. meetings. I was also doing Twelve Step Work, sharing my experience, strength, and hope with newcomers to the program. I felt like a hypocrite. I felt that I was trying to live two lives. Suddenly I became very sick and had a hard job running the business. Finally I went to the Civic Hospital, where they took x-rays and told me that I had pneumonia. They kept me in hospital and put me on antibiotics. It cleared up in a week or so, but I still felt weak.

I was getting short of cash. I was in touch with my son, Mike, in Montreal, and he loaned me a thousand dollars. This did a lot for my morale, and also made me happy to know that he trusted me. Michael was always such a good kid. I'll always regret not getting to know him as he grew up, but right then I just wanted to sell the business and to live the A.A. program.

I had been sitting on the fence leading a double life but now I had a choice to make—I could either continue to set up scams and swindle people, or I could get honest with myself and practice the program—take inventory, and try to give back some of the beautiful things that I had received. I decided there were to be no more games.

My next move was to sell the business for whatever I could get for it and concentrate on my recovery. A woman wanted to become a partner so I made a deal with her. She paid me the money that I had invested up to then, along with a couple of thousand to pay off outstanding debts. Also there was a lawyer, a good friend whom I had gone to see, and he agreed to take the two thousand and pay the bills after I left. This was a big step in the right direction for me and it made me feel good. Over a year later he sent me a cheque for $308 and an itemized list of the bills he had paid.

There were times when I thought of myself as a sucker and doubted my sanity, but getting out of the business really was the biggest step I had taken until then on my road to recovery. It was moves like this that I continued to make that brought me some measure of self-respect. The long hard struggle was starting to pay off. If I could continue to make the right moves and let go, and let God help, I knew that I would continue to recover.

CHAPTER ELEVEN

THE LONG ROAD BACK

I n retrospect, I have discovered that the unveiling of more and more defects is the most discouraging aspect. At first I thought that my biggest problems were alcohol and drugs, but they were only the tip of the iceberg.

When I stopped drinking alcohol and using drugs, I had to take a good look at myself inside and out. What I found was enough garbage to sink a battleship! No wonder I had become my own worst enemy. My worst defects were fear, hate, ignorance, self-deception, paranoia and anger.

I had come to believe that the many times people in authority had thrown me into solitary confinement, padded cells, dead locks, straightjackets, and leg-irons was because they didn't like me. I discovered that they used all these restraints because they had no choice.

Today I know that joining the A.A. program was the best thing that ever happened to me because it forced me to take a good, long, honest look at myself. I had to stop conning and rationalizing my actions. That may sound easy, but it was the most difficult new habit that I ever attempted. The way I see it, being honest with myself must continue to be my top priority. I am trying to achieve a new set of values that will continually increase my faith, happiness, serenity and quality of life. When I focus on what is good today, I have a good day; when I focus on what is bad, I have a bad day. If I focus on a problem, the problem increases. If I focus on the answer, the answer increases.

One thing I am grateful for is that if I had known the extent of the brain damage from which I was trying to recover, I am sure I would not have even tried.

Acceptance is the key to my relationship with God, for my serenity is directly proportional to my level of acceptance. When I remember this, I can see that I have never had it so good. Thank God for this wonderful program. For so long I could not distinguish between religion and spirituality. I dreaded the thought of getting religious. I had always found religious people very boring, especially when they talked about God, or when they preached to me. Now I understand spirituality to be faith in action. You don't tell them, you show them—a good example is worth a thousand words. You cannot help a desperate, hopeless man or woman by preaching at them. You must learn to listen to them. Let them use you as a sounding board to relieve themselves of their frustrations and pain. It is better to understand than to be understood.

When I call on a desperate person today, I try to make a connection, sharing or relating similar experiences. When they realize that I know how they feel, that I have been down the same old road and that there is a better way to live, I simply plant the seed and pray that it will grow in them. This is known in our program as a Twelve Step call. It is carrying the message. There cannot be an unsuccessful Twelve Step call, because even if the person does not respond to our efforts to help, there are many benefits received for just trying to be helpful. It is so true when A.A. members say that to keep the program you have to give it away. We share our experience, strength and hope with the newcomer and with one another. It is a beautiful design for living that works in everyday life.

The facts are that we have had deep and effective spiritual experiences that have changed our whole attitude towards life.

These experiences were what I needed to affect my first conscious relationship with God as I understood Him. Afterwards, I found myself accepting many things that formerly were out of reach. That was growth for me, but if I wished to grow I had to begin somewhere, so I used my own conception of God, however limited it was.

I needed to ask myself but one short question, "Do I now believe, or am I even willing to believe?" As soon as I became willing to believe, and when I saw others solve their problems by a simple reliance upon the spirit of the universe, my life started to change for the better. I had to stop doubting the power of God. My ideas did not work, but the God idea did.

I can honestly say that the greatest fight, the most important opportunity for a good and happy life, came my way as a result of being introduced to the Twelve Steps. I have put these steps to full use in my everyday life, and the benefits I have received are unbelievable.

Not only did I experience a spiritual awakening as the result of these steps, but the results are still coming in. I have recovered from alcohol and drugs, my sobriety and sanity have returned to a higher level than ever before. I now measure my mental health and sobriety by how good I feel. Do I get my share of laughs out of each day? Am I happy? Do I have many friends? Do I get along with people? Am I invited out? What is my attitude to all this? It has become tremendously important for me to accept the things I cannot change in this world. I have a new set of values, and, above all, a new and stronger faith in God, who gives me the courage to change. These new habits give me self-esteem, which I need to be happy.

I define mental health as the adjustment of human beings to the world and to one another with a maximum of effectiveness and happiness. Not just efficiency, or contentment, or the grace of obeying the rules of the game cheerfully, but all of these together. Mental health is the ability to maintain an even temper, an alert intelligence, socially considerate behaviour and a happy disposition. A "healthy mind," I discovered through the Twelve Steps, is my greatest asset today. My happiness depends upon the quality of my thinking. I arrived in this program with grave emotional and mental disorders and my thinking only brought me pain. Now, at this moment, I am so grateful to have been given the chance to live again.

I have found a way to replace my despair with hope, my paranoia with a trust in God and man, my depression with a full and active life as a therapist and counsellor. The program also changed my hate to love.

I remember going on retreats every two months at the Trappist monastery at Oka, Quebec. The first time they asked me why I was there I answered that I was not too sure, but that lately I was reading books that people had recommended, but I did not understand or enjoy them. Also I was associating with religious people, which really turned me off. I was confused and wondered if I was on the right track. The monastery may be the last place on earth where I would expect to find myself, but I had promised to go to any length to get sane and sober, so there I was.

On a later retreat they again asked me why I came. I told them it was to work on a couple of defects of character. When I was leaving they asked me if I had found what I had come for. I responded that I thought I got gypped, because I had come with two defects of character and now had four. As we continue to take personal inventory we find more and more defects.

Many other programs have evolved out of the original Alcoholics Anonymous, or along similar lines. There is Al-Anon, Al-Ateen, Narcotics Anonymous, Cocaine Anonymous, Gamblers Anonymous, Overeaters Anonymous, and many others. There are well over two million people who have recovered and can bear witness that the Twelve Step program really does work, and can eliminate any major problem from their lives, be it drugs, alcohol, gambling, or sex. It's for anyone who wants a new philosophy of life, a positive and healthy attitude, self-respect, happiness or self-esteem. This new way of life is yours if you have the guts to accept the challenge and put twelve simple steps into your life. I thought that life would be terribly boring if I cleaned up my act, but in fact it is getting more exciting as I continue meeting the challenge of a great new life.

Many years ago, I came across a story titled *Your Ignorance Is Showing*. My vocabulary then was straight from the gutter and I could not speak without using filthy language, mostly four letter words. I had no respect for anyone; I was full of hate. And whatever friends I had, used the same type of language. The story said that people were considered ignorant if they used this type of language. For a long time I couldn't have cared less. But now, as I look back, I think that this book presented my first real challenge because I didn't want people to think I was ignorant.

I have been lucky in the things that I've heard and read. One night a very successful millionaire, a businessman, was being interviewed on TV. When asked what he considered to be his greatest asset, he answered, "That's simple. It is the quality of my thinking." That statement really impressed me because I could not help thinking that as I more or less force-fed myself with good books and the simple Twelve Steps through one ear, the garbage seemed to flow out the other. One day at a time I keep feeding my computer (my brain) a positive program and it keeps finding and destroying the old garbage.

I have been counselling addicts for many years and have worked in treatment centres, missions and jails. I'm also a member of the Canadian Association of Remotivation Therapists. I've travelled the road to recovery for over forty years. It has taken me to jails, mental hospitals, many treatment centres, and all types of programs. I believe my addiction to alcohol was apparent when I was about twelve years old. I later became addicted to drugs, sex, gambling, cigarettes, food. I joined Alcoholics Anonymous, Narcotics Anonymous, ACOA and many other programs.

Although I went to many psychiatrists, psychologists, counselors—well meaning people—many of them inflicted their own theories and ideas on me which left me more confused and frustrated than before. Dr. Fritz Perls, the well-known psychiatrist, referred to this as mind fucking. He used the term to show how some specialists put their ideas into other peoples' heads to explain their behaviour. Being an addict, I had to realize how futile it was to depend on others for the answers.

There were also many doctors, therapists, and counsellors, who could re-motivate an addict into joining a self-help program like A.A. or Narcotics Anonymous. It was one such doctor who convinced me that the most successful way to recover from an addiction was a program of Twelve Steps, where you could share experiences, strengths, and hope with one another. I must emphasize the importance of one day at a time.

The way a therapist handles your feelings of inadequacy is crucial to the cure, since your sense of worthlessness is a key to your addictions or depression. Neither love, nor approval, nor friendship, nor a capacity for close, caring, human relationships, add one iota to your inherent self-worth. The great majority of addicted individuals are, in fact, very much loved, but it doesn't help one bit because it is self-love and self-worth that determine how you feel: you feel the way you think.

Cognitive therapy can help us by changing the way we think—we can alter our moods, deal with emotional problems, and get rid of depression without the use of drugs. A thinking trap we often fall into is referred to as the "binocular trick" because you are either magnifying—blowing things up out of proportion—or minimizing—shrinking them out of proportion. Magnification commonly occurs when you look at your own errors, fears or imperfections and exaggerate their importance: "My God, I made a mistake—how awful! The word will spread like wildfire—my reputation is ruined!" You're looking at your faults through the end of the binoculars that makes them appear gigantic and grotesque. This phenomenon has also been called catastrophizing because common-place negative events are turned into nightmarish monsters. When you think about your strengths, you may do the opposite, looking through the other end of the binoculars so that things look small and unimportant. If you magnify your imperfections and minimize your good points, you are guaranteed to feel inferior.

But the problem *isn't you*—it's the crazy lenses you're wearing. I've had tremendous results with my friends and my clients by introducing them to this new way of thinking, and the change from being their own worst enemy to their own best friend is amazing. As their point of view becomes positive, the quality of their relationships and/or marriage improves. There are also improvements in the quality of their friendships, their health, and their life.

Recently, I had the pleasure of presenting a five-year medallion to my friend and sponsee, Rick, for five years of sobriety. Rick is the vice-president of a computer company and his beautiful wife and proud children were there to celebrate his anniversary. It was hard to believe that just five years ago he had been a member of a motorcycle gang in Montreal. Now he is a good father, husband, friend, example, and is completely free of his addictions.

There are so many more people like Rick, who have recovered from their addictions, who are now successful, responsible, and above all, happy human beings. You too can find the courage to change with a simple Twelve Step program. This program teaches us to depend not on another, but to lean instead on thyself. True happiness is born of self-reliance. As a Remotivation Therapist, I try to help by encouraging clients to find, understand,

and to get to the roots of their problems and deal with them. This should become a new habit that increases in value every day of your life.

I have to tell you how I stopped smoking after the cancer scare, when I had controlled the amount of my smoking for a time. I was determined to stop as soon as I left the hospital, so I bought some books on how to stop smoking. Then, I made an appointment with a hypnotist—I stopped for one hour. Then there was the acupuncturist—that was good for another hour. Then I tried Smokers Anonymous, nicotine gum, straw cigarettes. But, I could not stop as I had no willpower.

There were many people who had told me that they had prayed to God to remove the compulsion to smoke—and it had worked. I decided to walk into an old Franciscan church in Montreal to pray. My prayer went something like this "God, I know I should have come here first but I went to the hypnotist, acupuncturist, Smokers Anonymous, and read lots of books on how to stop smoking and nothing works, so could you please remove my compulsion to smoke." I left that church and have never had a cigarette since. And I've never wanted one—like the compulsion for alcohol, drugs, and other addictions, the compulsion to smoke has gone!

Before my attempts at returning to sanity, I had been put under lock and key in solitary confinement, dead-lock, padded cells, straitjackets, handcuffs, leg-irons, all of which were supposed to rehabilitate me, but the truth was that each incarceration increased my insanity. My return to sanity and common sense took longer than I thought, because I was so messed up and I had so many hang-ups as a result of my more than twenty addictions, beginning with alcohol, drugs, tobacco, gambling, needles, lying, stealing, fear, anger, self-deception, self-destruction, misery, self-centeredness, denial, resentment, paranoia, criticism, ignorance, manipulation, control, and hate.

The reform schools taught me about sexual perversion, fear, cruelty, frustration, confusion, and many lessons in how to escape. What I did not know at the time was that I was becoming a victim of the system and was being force-fed toxic information and examples of how to lie, cheat, steal, swindle, con, manipulate, and control. A whole new set of tools that would be so self-destructive.

When they lock your cell and the lights go out, and good dreams are dead and gone, you are left with only the garbage in your head. Albert

Einstein's theory was that as you upgrade the quality of your thinking, your problems seem to disappear. When I used to think sick and depressing thoughts, I deserved to get what I always got—sick and depressing results. So I took my power back and used self-discipline to eliminate destructive thoughts. When I don't think of a drink; I don't have a drink, when I don't think of a drug or cigarette; I don't have a drug or cigarette.

Insanity is defined as a deranged state of the mind and I could well understand my emotional and mental disorders as the result of an alcoholic father who terrorized his fifteen children. I was the fourteenth. I came to accept fear as a basic ingredient of life and learned to live with it. I ran away from home at the age of seven to escape the fears, terror and hopelessness of my existence. I began to steal bread and milk at the doorsteps to fill my hunger for food. But there were many other hungers that I had that I could not understand at that time.

I had a great hunger for love and understanding, warmth, comfort, knowledge, friendship, hope, faith, a place to relax and get my bearings, a place to try to rewrite the script. I discovered many years later the quality or state of being tranquil. There was so much to learn and so much to unlearn.

I was very fortunate in discovering what God could do for me. This was one of many obstacles I had to face. My Mother was a believer who went to church every day and she was run over by a bus. So from my personal experiences, I felt he was no friend of mine. But I had to admit that the people who were practicing the Twelve Steps of Alcoholics Anonymous were a lot happier, more responsible and recovering much faster than I was. I was so impressed I began to fake it and let on that I had come to believe. Then came a day when I did not have to fake it anymore. Common sense told me that the more steps and spiritual thoughts I stuffed into my head the more garbage was released. I also had to admit that I was feeling so much better. I was singing in the morning, laughing more than ever and trying to pass it on to whoever would listen.

I had been doing time in a lot of jails and skid road dives and mental hospitals. Now I found myself doing time in schools and libraries, searching out people who could upgrade my thinking.

At discussion meetings in A.A., I was afraid to open my mouth at first for fear my ignorance would show. But as I began to upgrade my education, improve my vocabulary, and upgrade my thinking, I was free to give my opinion and they seemed to ask more questions. This was really good for my self-esteem. I was truly becoming responsible and accountable for my actions and my thoughts. I was becoming very excited about my new interests and change of life.

I can very well remember trying to read the Big Book put out by Alcoholics Anonymous, and other self-help books, and I read the same page four or five times trying to understand what the words meant. I became so frustrated, and cursed those who used words that I had to look up in the dictionary. Afterwards I began to carry a pocket-sized dictionary everywhere. When I decided to write this book, I tried to keep the message simple and write in words that anyone could understand because drugs, including alcohol, attack the brain.

I was fortunate to have found some great books on the *Power of Positive Thinking*, *Art of Thinking,* and a pamphlet written by Emmett Fox, author of *Sermon on the Mount*, and many other books. In this pamphlet I discovered a seven-day mental diet that really appealed to me because I had come to believe I was addicted to misery. I was prepared to go to any length to change my attitude. The diet consisted of watching my every word and not saying a single negative thing, or a mean or dishonest thing, or make any depressing remarks for seven days.

Now that is of course a big undertaking. I tried it one day and failed. I tried it again and again, and then made two days before I slipped. I tried many times without success. I asked God to help me for I knew I just had to change myself, or else. I stayed home and finally succeeded to get four days, and the next attempt I completed the seven days. Not once for seven days did I fail. Then I thought it would be okay to go back to my old ways, but I found that there was a difference within myself. Actually I could not go back. I was changed, not completely, of course, but I was not the same person. Since then life has become different. Now I am always aware of my thoughts and my thinking, which I try to choose very carefully.

After searching for so many years in all the wrong places, institutions, doctors, therapists, counsellors, pills of all kinds, I finally discovered it was an inside job, recognized the truth, and got honest with myself. I came to believe that God is not the enemy; he is a true friend who will never let me down. My greatest source of strength is my God. All I have to do is keep the faith, and pass it on. This can also be your solution—ask him for help and he will be there for you.

CHAPTER TWELVE

THE GREATEST HIGH OF THEM ALL

I sought my soul, my soul I could not see,
I sought my God, my God eluded me,
I sought my brother, and I found all three.

When I am asked how I know there is a God, I answer I have been to Hell. In Hell there is nothing but fear, terror, hate, rage, insanity, evil and death. My situation had become so hopeless that any change was better than the way it was and I finally realized that I had to try to find a way out.

I got into drugs and alcohol to assist me in ignoring and escaping my problems, my suffering, and my fears. By deadening myself to the pain I could forget the problems that caused the pain. However, alcohol—the solution I had found that would relieve me of my fears—finally betrayed me and made my fears worse.

For many years I would not accept responsibility for my problems. I had become really good at conning and believing my own lies. There was always someone else to blame for my problems: my wife, my friends, the reform schools, jails, mental hospitals, society and "the system." But I heard somewhere that if I was not part of the solution then I was part of the problem. As I moved up the Twelve Steps, I came to realize that no problem can be solved until I assume responsibility for solving it.

Life is full of pain as well as joy. It is in the process of facing and solving problems, and overcoming the pain, that life has meaning. Problems do not go away. They must be worked through or else they remain forever a barrier to the growth and development of the spirit. As I try to achieve mental and spiritual health, I need to face my problems directly, and to experience the pain involved.

Discipline provides a basic set of tools we require to solve life's problems. When I teach myself discipline, I am teaching myself how to bear the pain and how to grow. Yet when one is dedicated to the truth, the pain seems relatively unimportant. And it also gets less and less painful the farther one proceeds on the path of self-examination. My purpose in life today is to grow to be the most that I am capable of being—sometimes it is painful, most of the time it is joyful.

Albert Einstein had a theory that as you raise the quality of your thinking, you will raise the quality of your life and your problems will seem to disappear. In my addicted state, I was incapable of making good decisions or the right choices for myself, and my problems seemed to multiply. But when I was given help in making good decisions and good choices, my life began to improve and more important, I felt much better. I began to realize the value of positive thinking.

My brain did not have the capacity to hold more than one thought at a time, so as my brain was receiving more and more good thoughts, there became less and less room for my old ideas and sick thinking. The results of upgrading my thinking, my education, my vocabulary, and my frame of mind, began to pay off in better decisions and better choices.

As the quality of my thinking got better, so did the quality of my life. I actually started to feel good. In fact, better than I ever felt before. This convinced me that I was on the right track. Today, it is so important to me to continue to improve the quality of my thinking. I believe that I am what I think.

For years I had been a skeptic and would often make fun of people who had come to believe in

God, saying that they were being brainwashed and believed in fairy tales. But as I worked to improve the quality of my thinking, I realized I needed something more to get over my addictions and change my life. I looked around for people that I wanted to emulate. I saw that people who were practicing the Twelve Steps of Alcoholics Anonymous and believed in God were the happiest people. They had courage and confidence in themselves. They could get up in front of a crowd and always say the right thing. They definitely had more patience and tolerance. Last, but not least, they were going through a personality change. It was like watching a caterpillar change into a beautiful butterfly before my eyes.

I wanted what they had, to be the way they were. I saw that to make real progress I had to have faith. This was easier said than done. How the hell do you get faith? All I can suggest is what I did: fake it until you make it. Without really knowing whom I was talking to, or what I expected, I started with a simple prayer of "Please, God, help me."

What really confused and held back my progress was my belief that religion and faith were one and the same. To me, "religion" was the memory of my father, who would come home drunk on

Saturday night, throw my Mother down the stairs and beat us kids. Then on Sunday morning this pious, holier-than-thou maniac would walk down the aisle of the church looking like a saint, and kneel at the altar for Holy Communion. Then there were times I felt I was no better when I would surrender my life to Jesus and make a spectacle of myself at different churches, just to get a ticket for food and relieve my hunger pains.

I knew my Mom had a beautiful faith, but even though she was a living example that faith worked, I couldn't believe. When my Mom was run over by the bus, I cursed God and swore that I would have nothing else to do with Him.

Much later in my life of self-examination, I realized that at that time one of my defects helped me. I was stubborn. But for once in my life, my stubbornness paid off. I kept going back to A.A. meetings, and although I could not digest the speaker's words or the laughter, I knew there was something there and I was determined to keep coming back until I found out what it was. I remember thinking, "If them bastards can laugh and be happy, so can I."

I had once been given the nickname, "Mike, the actor," and any ability I might have had for acting came into good use in my program. I decided to play their game, to look and act like I was one of them. Whenever they said something that sounded intelligent, I would steal their lines. Little did I know, there were advantages in doing what I was doing: if you play a part long enough you can actually become that person.

I began asking for faith and for some sign that He was hearing me. At this time, I had a beautiful little Lhasa Apso, named Tiger, who had a mind of his own. I tried to train him but I think he ended up training me. We became real close and he even showered with me.

Each morning I would take him on a walk. We would often walk to the park on the corner, which was called Pigeon Park because there were always lots of pigeons there and he loved chasing them. On one particular morning my thoughts were on faith. As I was walking out the door, for some reason, I stopped on the lawn, looked skyward, and said, "God, I am willing to go to any length to try and straighten out my life and attempt to repair the damage I have caused myself and others. If you are up there and can hear me could you please give me a sign or some message that could help me to believe."

By this time Tiger was going crazy wanting to get going. As we approached the park Tiger began his usual wild and ferocious actions. He would bark and jump two or three feet in the air and growl, scaring every pigeon in sight. There would be a couple of hundred birds one minute, and none the next.

You can imagine my surprise on this morning when one bird didn't take off. I held the leash up near Tiger's head and walked toward the bird to see if it was hurt and I could help it. First I bent down and patted it then I put my hand under its breast and carried it back to a bench a hundred feet away. I sat with the bird on my left side, Tiger on my right. I was very surprised that Tiger was so quiet. I don't think I had ever seen him this calm. I said to Tiger, "This bird must have a broken wing. We will take him home and see if we can fix his wing so that he can fly again."

Suddenly the bird just flew away. As it got smaller and smaller in the distance, I remembered my short prayer to God to please give me a sign to help me to believe in faith. It sure made me think, if that beautiful little bird could have faith in Tiger and me, why couldn't I have faith in a higher power?

Since that day, my concept of God has continued to change and grow along with the quality of my life and happiness. At first I did not want anyone to know that I believed in God. I worried about what "they" would say. Maybe "they" would not like me. But with some of my new-found courage and clearer thinking, I started saying, Who the hell are they? Why the hell should I worry about what they might think or what they might say? It took me a while to find a God of my understanding, and to believe that He really is there for everyone who believes, but I have found faith to be the solution to all my addictions. It can be yours too.

There was a time when I thought A.A. was all bullshit and that I would be bored to death if I followed their directions. Today I know that the A.A. program is what pulled me through, and I will never be able to express the immense gratitude that I have for that beautiful fellowship and all the great people who stuck by me.

A.A. is a simple program that I tried to complicate in every way. When I accepted that I was the problem, that I was very sick, and I finally asked God for help, my recovery started. It took me fifteen years to get a one-year cake, but I feel very fortunate because there are many who never accomplish that.

I had to be willing to go to any lengths, and that included the Twelve Steps. First, I became willing to get serious about managing my life. On the second step, I came to believe that a power greater than myself could return me to sanity. On the third step, I made a decision to turn my will and my life over to the care of God as I understood him. On the fourth step, I began looking for my problems and began dealing with them.

For the first twelve or thirteen years that I stopped drinking I was bitter, and resented that I could not drink as other people did. I was what they call a "dry drunk," miserable as hell and getting meaner all the time. There were many answered prayers, but I couldn't see any benefits.

My sponsor told me that I was taking a lot for granted. He asked when I had had my last drink, and if I liked the business I had. He also mentioned my good health, the fine women I had, the money in the bank, the self-respect, and respect of my children and he made me realize that the many gifts that had come my way were probably the result of my prayers, but that I did not seem to appreciate very much.

He explained to me how very important it was to be grateful, and as he spoke, something I had heard in my travels came to mind: happiness is not found in having what you want, but in wanting what you have. I had to learn to appreciate my new gifts, so I started praying for a grateful heart, and soon learned the value of gratitude. My faith and my happiness seemed to increase as I became more grateful for what I had and for my successes. You cannot be grateful and unhappy at the same time.

Abraham Lincoln once said: "You can be as happy as you make up your mind to be." It is so true. My happiness is in direct proportion to how diligently I practice and live my program—my course in miracles!

I can express my love now in sharing, caring, consideration, respect, and understanding. The sad part of it is that some of the people I share this love with don't even know that they are being loved, but I remember that this same type of love was given so freely to me at one time, and that it only confused me because I could not recognize it either. But now I am sure that it was love that made me realize I had to change and kept me coming back to A.A. and the Twelve Steps.

When I think that this beautiful high that I am on won't cost me any money or give me a hangover, and that I can stay this high, through love and the grace of God, for as long as the quality of my thinking remains high, I see the power that positive thinking has.

I was asked to share my experience, strength and hope at an A.A. group meeting at the Douglas Hospital (a mental hospital where I had previously been locked up as a patient). I met a couple of the old patients that I had done time with, and when I went back to give a talk at the Douglas Hospital, they said "We knew you'd be back!" I have also spoken in jails and penitentiaries across the country, even in places I did time.

How great it was to walk in and out of these establishments a free man! I have finally come to know what freedom really is; I'm not just free of the jails but free of my old attitude, free of my old thinking, free of my worst enemy—my sick mind.

Today my life is great, and getting better all the time. A few years ago I received a diploma as a Remotivation Therapist, after being a student and working as a group therapist at the Douglas Hospital.

Then, in 1988, I received a letter from the House of Commons—I was sure that it was some type of a practical joke. The letter invited me to a dinner in the Railway Committee Room on March 23, 1988. Following this I got a lovely card in the mail that said the Speaker of the Senate and Speaker of the House of Commons, on behalf of the Parliamentary Breakfast Group, requested the pleasure of my company at the 23rd Annual National Prayer Breakfast with members of the Cabinet, members of the Supreme Court and other national leaders on March 24, 1988, in the Confederation Room. There was also another luncheon that afternoon and I was asked to speak.

I spoke on the many hungers I had known: the hunger for food that made me steal milk and bread, and led me to reform school; the hunger for love that my wonderful Mom tried to give to me. I spoke of the hunger for knowledge, the hunger for spiritual health, the hunger for human dignity and self-respect. I spoke of the way I found to satisfy my different hungers with the help of God, which for me is the only way.

The memory of those two days in Ottawa will always be great, but what really put the icing on the cake was knowing that my Mother would be proud of me, and that she was right in her prediction—that I would turn out all right in the end.

MY DO IT
YOURSELF PROGRAM

I have told you what it was like, what happened and what it is like now. There are not enough hours in a day to do all the things I would like to do. My greatest wish in telling my story is that it will reach others who feel desperate, hopeless, and lonely because of their problems and addictions.

Alcoholic's Anonymous gives us a program: the Twelve Steps. It is suggested that we accept the medicine, since it gets to taste better all the time. Put the steps into your life and you will find a design for living and a new freedom and happiness that you have never known.

My Do It Yourself Program to overcome drug and alcohol addictions works. You will have to work at it by choosing to take inventory—use self-discipline, become self-reliant, and use self-restraint. Also by becoming responsible and accountable for your thoughts and actions.

Then, part of your recovery requires you to pass it on to other unfortunate alcoholics or drug addicts. Faith without works is dead, if we want to keep what we have, we have to give it away. We try to give them a little hope and get them to their first A.A. meeting. There are newcomers who wonder why they keep coming back. We give them hope and love with no strings attached, and in return our own faith increases and we experience a new and wonderful high.

In Ottawa I started a Twelve Step meeting that was open to anyone who wanted help at solving their problems and finding a new way of life. There are now two other Twelve Step groups that have sprung from this group. We also started another group for adult children of alcoholics, who have very similar, and in some cases, more serious problems than the alcoholics themselves. These children have a higher risk than usual of becoming alcoholics and can end up with many problems, but through practicing the Twelve Steps they, too, can become healthy and happy.

My greatest ambition is to introduce this successful program to the inmates of jails and penitentiaries across the country, so that they may also have a chance at the good life. I was never rehabilitated in the reform schools or the many prisons I was in. They only made me worse. A.A. in prisons would be a low-cost program that would produce great results.

At present there are many prisons that allow A.A. meetings once a week, and the results have been great, but if the program was an integrated part of a rehabilitation program it would do wonders for the morale and mental health of the inmates. It could be introduced as a course in how to live. The Twelve Steps are the greatest therapy for a new and happy life. There is lots of proof that the program works: For example, former inmates like myself who speak at A.A. meetings, telling how they were first introduced to A.A., how they never had to return to prison, and how good life is today.

There are some who say that life begins at forty but for me life began when I accepted a God of my understanding. This became the greatest adventure of my life and it will never end.

MY OPINION ON MARIJUANA

I want to speak out against the publicity surrounding legalizing marijuana—in my opinion, you might as well be opening the gates to all drugs, and legalizing insanity. For many years I was a user of marijuana, which I will refer to as "pot," and I know this is a mind-altering drug that some people claim is harmless or good for you. I believe this should be called a disease of denial nurtured by the use of this drug.

Anyone who has a healthy mind should be able to admit and accept the fact that *any* smoking is unhealthy. To get the most out of pot, you have to take a big drag on the joint and hold the smoke in your lungs so that it will give you the most "effective" results.

When I hear or read about people who use it for medical reasons, I can understand how easy it would be for them to believe that it's helping them. At one time I, too, was convinced that it was harmless and even helping me. It made me feel good and laugh more, and took me on a trip that released me from responsibilities, accountabilities, worries, and inhibitions. When I smoked a joint, I thought I was able to justify anything I said or did.

My personal experiences with this drug led me to other drugs. The next step for me was "if one is good, two is better." Then I began to change the recipe—adding some hash, amphetamines, coke—always trying to get the most bang for my buck! It truly was an escape from reality. My life had been so troubled and miserable and so full of fear, I became fully convinced that this was the best medicine I had ever found for what ailed me and it was easy to believe that this was my elixir to a wonderful life. Chapter ten explains where this elixir really led me.

I have been a salesman or con man most of my life and I had become a professional liar. I found the truth is the hardest thing to sell. I have heard and read so much about the pro's and con's of marijuana. But I know from personal experience that although it did give me a short escape from hell, marijuana was just a step down into the dungeon of my self-destruction.

The reality of my life now is truth and honesty, without deception. When I began to recognize and accept the truth and became honest with myself without drugs, I also found the greatest high of them all.

SAMPLES FROM SURVIVORS IN RECOVERY KIT

I have included in this appendix some samples of poems, quotes and thoughts that inspired me in my recovery. I have been asked many times by my sponsees and clients to make up a kit of all the items like these that would help them to concentrate on what is important in their recovery. So I created the Survivors in Recovery Kit, which includes these poems, quotes, stories and thoughts as well as recordings on your choice of two tapes or CDs.

At the end of this appendix is an order form for the Survivors in Recovery Kit, with information for ordering the Kit, or the Kit plus *The Road to Hell...and Back* book. You can order by mail, phone, fax or email. Our price includes shipping and handling.

MY DAYS AS AN
ASSISTANT RABBI

I could never understand why Rabbi Eli
Gottesman took an interest in me, an Irish
Catholic. I had been on the streets since the
age of seven when I left home. As I added alcohol
and drugs to my already sick mind, I became a
wild animal. The brothers and priests at the reform
school I first attended, were supposed to be repre-
senting God and nearly killed me with their
beatings. One time I went to a Catholic church for
confession, and when I was through, the priest told
me that if I ever came back with another confession like that, he would call the police and have me
arrested. I was flabbergasted at such treatment
from a priest!

I can't recall how I met the rabbi. I was at my
worst as an active alcoholic and drug addict, and I

was always looking for ways to support my addictions and my family, when I met this man who was the complete opposite to me in every way. He was the rabbi of the Beth Aaron Synagogue in Montreal. He had his doctorate degree, and I had been expelled from every school I ever attended, even reform school. He also had been a colonel in the American Air Force during the Second World War and acted as an advisor or consultant to the officers and enlisted men who sought spiritual help. So when I met this rabbi, I might say I was a little surprised and thought it strange when he asked me for my help.

I later came to believe that it was reverse psychology. He knew I had a wife and kids to support and wanted me to believe that I was useful. He raised my self-worth and at the time I really thought that I was a help to him. I must admit I was still playing games, but the truth was he gave me a hunger for knowledge and an opportunity to escape my misery and ignorance. I had what you might call "street smarts," I was always trying to find a person's weakness and take advantage of it. His weakness was that he was very forgetful. One Friday morning after he had given me my pay for the week, he then gave it to me again, forgetting that I was already paid. I later took advantage of this by asking for my pay a second time and I received it. I justified this by thinking he was making so much money he would not miss it.

Dr. Gottesman had received his doctorate in literature, and he was in the final stages of completing two big books. One was a reference book about the past two hundred years of Jewish life in Canada. The other book was *Who's Who in Canadian Jewry*. We were soon on a first name basis. Eli was very shy so I became his assistant, or front man, helping him with his interviews with prominent Canadian businessmen such as Charles and Ed Bronfman and other outstanding leaders of the community.

I can remember thinking we must have appeared as a very odd couple. I had introduced myself as Michael Maloney, but out of respect for Eli I changed my name to Michael Mendleson and I began to wear a *yarmulke* and talk with a Jewish accent! Whenever I arrived at the synagogue early, he would always say "already so soon!" so I adopted that saying. Then I would use words like *shalom* and other Jewish words.

I began to try and act like he did and also started to nod a lot during interviews to show that I agreed with what they were saying—even though I didn't understand a word. I soon became accepted and began attending events at the synagogue. Eli helped me to stop drinking at the time, although I was still smoking a joint now and then.

He made the mistake of inviting me to a bar mitzvah. I had refused to go many times, but I finally agreed and was amazed at the amount of liquor being consumed. I refused a drink on two or three occasions at this particular bar mitzvah but I finally succumbed to the temptation and from what I heard when I came to, the party had really come alive after that. I began dancing with all the good-looking women and, as any good alcoholic knows, all women begin to look beautiful after that first drink. All I can remember was that I was dancing up a storm with a beautiful woman who seemed to be enjoying it as much as I was when this jerk kept trying to cut in. I got so mad I pulled his beard. Later after I woke up, I learned that he was only trying to retrieve his wife, and I had kept yelling at him to go find another woman and leave mine alone!

Eli would always make excuses for me but to my surprise, nobody seemed to be mad and they all thought it was very funny. The father of the bar mitzvah boy said it was the first time they had seen someone try to steal a man's wife at a Bar Mitzvah.

They were all shocked at the way the husband had struck me and dragged the woman across the floor. She sure wasn't much to look at after he got through with her! I guess the moral of this story is never to invite an Irish alcoholic to a bar mitzvah.

There were so many funny and strange situations in which we found ourselves. We would stop for lunch at a restaurant and I would order a good meal while he would just order a cup of weak tea and a slice of lemon. The waitress could never understand why my side of the table would be nice and clean while Eli's side would be littered with crumbs. The reason was he would carry a couple of hard rolls in his pocket, because he could not eat the restaurant food since it was not kosher.

He introduced me to a new way of life that I came to really appreciate in later years. I am sure that he made a much better man of me, and made me realize the importance of education, knowledge, and the quality of my thinking. It was because of his example that I later returned to school.

In those days I was always complaining about my wife, saying that she wasn't beautiful and that she was lazy. After asking me some questions, he got me to admit that she was a good wife and he would tell me, a beautiful wife is good for a year but a good wife is beautiful for all her life.

PRAYERS

The following prayers are tools I use to keep in touch with the God of my understanding. Use these and make your own too.

One of the tools I use is the Serenity Prayer, which has helped me very much over the years: God grant me the serenity to accept the things I cannot change, the courage to change the things I can, and the wisdom to know the difference.

Each morning I thank God for my new, wonderful life. I remember how good it is to be alive, how grateful I am for my health, for my sobriety, for my sanity, for my friends and loved ones, for my new attitude of gratitude, for the smiles and laughter that come so easily, for the chance to sing again. I ask for God's help during the day. Each night I thank Him for my sobriety.

Please, God, don't ever let me become complacent or take anything for granted. I will be forever grateful for all my new and beautiful gifts, and hope to show my gratitude by trying to pass them on. May I always "remember when," so that I can appreciate more, each moment of this day.

IN ANGER

When I have lost my temper
I have lost my reason too.
I'm never proud of anything
Which angrily I do.

When I have talked in anger
And my cheeks are flaming red,
I have always uttered something
That I wish I hadn't said.

In anger I have never done
A kindly deed or wise,
But many things for which I know
I should apologize.

In looking back across my life
And all I've lost or made,
I can't recall a single time
When fury ever paid.
                    —Unknown

Principles Before Personalities

By centring our lives on correct principles we create a solid foundation for development of the four life-support factors.

♦ Our security comes from knowing that, unlike other centres based on people or things that are subject to frequent and immediate change, correct principles do not change. We can depend on them.

♦ Principles don't react to anything. They do not get mad and treat us differently. They will not divorce us. They cannot pave our way with shortcuts and quick fixes. They don't depend on the behaviour of others, the environment, or the current fad for their validity. Principles don't die. They are not here one day and gone the next. They cannot be destroyed by fire, earthquake or theft.

◆ Principles are deep, fundamental truths, classic truths, generic common denominators.

◆ They are tightly interwoven threads, which run with precision, consistency, beauty, and strength through the fabric of life. Even in the midst of people or circumstances that seem to ignore the principles, we can be secure in the knowledge that principles are bigger than people or circumstances, and that thousands of years of history have seen them triumph, time and time again.

◆ Even more important! We can be secure in the knowledge that we can validate them in our own lives, by our own experience.

◆ Admittedly we are not too smart. Our knowledge and understanding of correct principles is limited by our own lack of awareness of our true nature and the world around us, and by the flood of trendy philosophies and theories that are not in harmony with correct principles.

◆ These ideas will have their season of acceptance, but like many before them, they won't endure because they are built on false foundations. We are limited, but we can push back the borders of our limitations. An understanding of the principle of our own growth enables us to search our correct principles with the confidence that the more we learn the more clearly we can focus the lens through which we see the world. The principles don't change; our understanding of them does.

♦ The wisdom and guidance that accompany principle-centred living comes from correct maps, from the way things really are, have been and will be. Correct maps enable us to clearly see where we want to go and how to get there. We can make our decisions using the correct data that will make their implementation possible and meaningful. The personal power that comes from principle-centred living is the power of a self-aware, knowledgeable, proactive individual, unrestricted by the attitudes, behaviours, and actions of others or by many of the circumstances and environmental influences that limit other people.

♦ The only real limitation of power is the natural consequences of the principles themselves. We are free to choose our actions based on our knowledge of correct principles, but we are not free to choose the consequences of those actions. Remember, if you pick up one end of the stick; you pick up the other.

♦ Principles always have natural consequences attached to them. There are positive conse-

quences when we live in harmony with the principles. There are negative consequences when
we ignore them, but because these principles
apply to everyone, whether or not they are
aware, this limitation is universal. The more we
know of correct principles, the greater is our
personal freedom to act wisely.

◆ By centring our lives on timeless, unchanging
   principles, we create a fundamental pattern of
   effective living.

◆ It is the centre that puts all other centres in
   perspective.

REPAIRS AND RENOVATIONS

My Do It Yourself Program, after so many years of neglect, mismanagement, self-deception and lies, and a diet of poisons, like alcohol, drugs, and tobacco, began when I sought help for my alcohol problems. I read the Big Book called Alcoholics Anonymous, which I could not understand too well, but which gave me the directions I would need to start repairing and renovating my body, mind, and soul. My body needed nutrition so that my brain could function better.

I began to change the steady diet of hamburgers, hot dogs, french fries and pasta, to fruits, vegetables, meats, and vitamins. I began to create a new pattern, and soon noticed that I had more energy and plain common sense. I then began to eliminate the poisons. Alcohol came first because it gave me the most problems. It was a disease of denial and very damaging to the brain. Abstinence allowed me the opportunity to recognize the most serious defects and damage I had created. One obstacle or challenge at a time had to be faced. My self-deception or bullshit wasn't working for me anymore. I had relieved myself of the lies by finding the truth. Telling myself, "I can't stop drinking, I can't stop using drugs, and I can't stop using tobacco"—this belief was allowing me to sabotage my health, my happiness, and my life.

Abraham Lincoln once said that you can be as happy as you make up your mind to be. This I've come to believe. Albert Einstein stated that as you raise the quality of your thinking and come to know the truth, your old problems will disappear. We have to change our old habits, our old attitudes, our old friends, and above all, our old beliefs.

In the year 2000, I received my twenty-five year medallion in Alcoholics Anonymous, also a twenty-five year medallion in Narcotics Anonymous. I can't shoot up anymore, or smoke up, or snort, pop pills or get drunk. But I sure can feel better than ever before. I laugh, sing, and wake up smiling. After so many jails, mental hospitals, treatment centres, skid row, the Old Brewery Mission in Montreal, the City Mission on Abbot Street in Vancouver, and after more than twenty addictions and my escape from Hell, I feel that you should understand my message. Get rid of "I can't," and say "If he can, I can." That is the truth, so believe it.

RECIPE FOR A COMPLETE RECOVERY

At first my return to sanity presented only a steady stream of obstacles, but somehow I knew I had to find the courage to face them. It is in this stage of recovery that we separate the men from the boys, and where we most need the support of fellow survivors. We start our list with a self-examination, or inventory, recognizing our most serious problems first—that is, our inability to abstain from the addictive and destructive behaviours that have been the source of all our difficulties. It is important to note that with persistence, and with the support of our fellow survivors, we will succeed one hour or even one minute at a time.

The priority list for my Recipe for Recovery was made up of the following ingredients:

- ◆ Self-examination (Inventory)
- ◆ Self-reliance
- ◆ Self-discipline
- ◆ Self-restraint
- ◆ Self-respect
- ◆ Self-conquest

Each case is different and we might have to adapt the list now and then, always keeping foremost in our minds that persistence really pays off. I switched my addictions completely from the poisonous substances and behaviors that were destroying me both physically and mentally, to the healthy "vitamins" for my body and soul that I now depend on today to nurture my full development as a human being.

The real challenge for me was to change my thinking from the negative to the positive by using "vitamins" for the mind—healthy thoughts. I believe you are what you think. One of my greatest discoveries was the realization that I had choices, and that I could choose to keep a thought or throw it out. I soon realized also that the greatest asset I could possess would be a quality of thinking that would guarantee me a new and wonderful life.

"Continue to think what you always thought,

and you'll continue to get what you always got," is an expression that was particularly apt in my case. My sick thinking told me that I could never change, that I was stuck forever in the depressed and miserable state of existence that I had created for myself. This is not true.

Once I rearranged my thinking and became aware of the value of self-discipline, self-restraint, self-reliance and the other important ingredients to a successful recovery, I did change. And I was able then to share with gratitude and love my experience, strength and hope with my fellow survivors.

Along the way, I also learned an important truth: In order to keep what I've found, I have to give it away. My Recovery Recipe is my gift to you, along with my sincere desire that you discover all the wonders that were so freely given to me.

OLD ADDICTIONS OR HABITS

1. My life was completely unmanageable and I assumed this was reality.
2. Could not believe and was too ignorant or stubborn to try.
3. Would not make the decision to turn it over, and laughed at those who did.
4. Could not take a searching and fearless moral inventory. I could not be fearless. I had no morals.
5. Could not admit to God, to myself or anyone else what I thought might be wrong. Did not believe there was a God.
6. Could not remove my defects and did not try. I thought they belonged with my lifestyle.
7. Did not know what a shortcoming was and could not see me as the problem.
8. Could not make a list of the people I had

harmed. I hated them, and was not willing.

9. Did not make any direct or indirect amends. Often used the words I'm sorry but did not mean it.

10. Could not take inventory and, when I was wrong, could not or would not admit it.

11. Could not relate to God, blamed Him for all my troubles.

12. Could not come to believe, make a decision to turn it over or accept a spiritual awakening, therefore I could not change or recover.

NEW ADDICTIONS OR HABITS

1. I believe that life is what I make it, and I try to manage it better each day.
2. I came to believe, and faith replaced my fears, alcohol, drugs, and insanity. It gave me a life.
3. Made the greatest decision of my life and escaped from Hell, to find God, love, my soul, my happiness.
4. Now I can live my Steps, and take a fearless and moral inventory of myself, and like what I find.
5. Admitted to God, to myself, and to other human beings, the exact nature of my wrongs. With the Twelve Steps I acquired a quality of thinking that has produced a quality, friends, faith, love, happiness, and life that I never thought possible.
6. Entirely ready to remove defects and

replace them with benefits, like patience, tolerance, respect, understanding, consideration, gratitude, faith, love.

7.   Humbly asked for removal of shortcomings.   Renew my decision morning and night.

8.   Made my list of people I had harmed.

9.   Made direct amends wherever possible and found that action speaks louder than words.

10.   Continued to take inventory and accept what I found.

11.   Improved my conscious contact with God as I understood him and became my own best friend.

12.   Having received a spiritual awakening and a very grateful heart, I try to carry my message to anyone who can keep an open mind and continue to pass it on.

KEEP GOING

There's no skill in easy sailing
When the skies are clear and blue.
There's no joy in merely doing
Things that anyone can do.

But there is great satisfaction,
That is mighty sweet to take,
When you reach a destination
That you said you couldn't make.

THINK YOU CAN

If you think you're beaten, you are;
If you think you dare not, you don't;
If you'd like to win, but think you can't,
It's almost a cinch you won't.

If you think you'll lose, you're lost,
For out in the world we find
Success begins with a fellow's **will**
It's all in the state of your mind.

If you think you're outclassed, you are;
You've got to think high to rise.
You've just got to be sure of yourself
Before you can win the prize.

Life's battles don't always go
To the stronger or faster man,
But sooner or later the man who wins
Is the one who **thinks he can!**

SURVIVORS IN RECOVERY KIT
ORDER FORM

I would like to order the Survivors Kit
including tapes or CDs

_____ copies @ $35.00 each $_____

Survivors Kit **with book,**
The Road to Hell...and Back

_____ copies @ $49.95 each $_____

GST (Canada only)
$2.63 or $3.75 w/book $_____

TOTAL AMOUNT ENCLOSED $_____

Check one: ☐CDs or ☐Tapes   *(Shipping and Handling Included)*

ORDERED BY:

NAME _____

ADDRESS _____

CITY _____ ZIP CODE _____

☐VISA ☐M/C EXP. DATE _____

CARD NUMBER _____

SIGNATURE _____

SHIP TO *(if different from above)*:

NAME _____

ADDRESS _____

CITY _____ ZIP CODE _____

PHONE: (_____) _____

Make checks payable to:

U.S.
Survivors in Recovery, Inc.
PO Box 1943
Blaine, WA 98231-1943

CANADA
Survivors in Recovery, Inc.
PO Box 63625
935 Marine Drive Unit 53
N. Vancouver, B.C. V7P 1S0

Orders accepted by Credit Card, Check or Money Order.
Please do not send cash
Credit card orders only: Phone: (800)555-6771
Fax: (604) 987-6710 EMail: maloney@uniserve.com